Vincentia Schroeter, Margit Koemeda-Lutz (Eds.)
Bioenergetic Analysis 2012 (22)

edition psychosozial

Vincentia Schroeter, Margit Koemeda-Lutz (Eds.)

Bioenergetic Analysis

The Clinical Journal of the International Institute for Bioenergetic Analysis (2012) Volume 22

Psychosozial-Verlag

Submissions for consideration
for the next volume of *Bioenergetic Analysis*
must be sent to the editor
(vincentiaschroeter@gmail.com)
between June and September, 2012.

Bibliographic information of the Deutsche Nationalbibliothek
(The German Library)
The Deutsche Nationalbibliothek lists this publication in
the Deutsche Nationalbibliografie; detailed bibliographic data
are available in the Internet at http://dnb.d-nb.de.

Original edition

E-Mail: info@psychosozial-verlag.de
www.psychosozial-verlag.de

Cover: Drawing of the Bioenergetic technique "towel pull sketch"
by Vincentia Schroeter
Draft design cover: Hanspeter Ludwig, Wetzlar
www.imaginary-art.net
Printed in Germany
ISBN 978-3-8379-2159-5

Contents

Reviewers for this issue were:

Nirmala Bhat

Peter Fernald

Margit Koemeda-Lutz

Mae Nasciemento

Tarra Stariell

Letter from the Editor

Dear Reader,

Welcome to the twenty-second edition of *Bioenergetic Analysis*, the clinical journal of the IIBA. The journal, as an arm of the IIBA would like to recognize and honor our venerable IIBA faculty who gained emeritus status in 2011. Each of them has trained generations of Bioenergetic therapists and put their unique stamp on this work. Thank you to Eleanor Greenlee, David Campbell, Marilyn Moranis, Vivian Guze and Bennett Shapiro.

The hard-working Board of Directors of the IIBA has decided to continue to offer this journal in print as a benefit to members, who appreciate a paper volume that they can hold in their hands. This 2012 edition contains five original articles, one poem and one book review.

As reflects our international flavor, we have papers that hail from New Zealand, the USA, Italy and Switzerland. Garry Cockburn discusses object relations and Bioenergetics in his article. Nicoletta Cinotti offers a paper on infant research. Bob Lewis presents a paper exploring if knowledge of neurobiology helps or hinders the clinical encounter. Helen Resneck provides a paper discussing the contributions of Harlow and Lowen in relation to neuroscience, attachment and love. Finally, Margit Koemeda discusses the latest data from neuroscience research and its implications for Bioenergetic clinicians.

These last three papers were keynote addresses at the October 2011 IIBA conference in San Diego. The theme of the conference was Neuroscience, the Mind and the Body. The exuberant conference opening was designed to celebrate the inclusiveness all the members. Thirty-four flags draped one wall at the conference, indicating the many countries that IIBA members come from. In the spirit of international communication, the journal offers translations of the abstracts of these papers into the five primary languages beside English. Thanks go to the translators. They are France Kauffman, Fina Pla, Mae Nasciemento, Jörg Clauer, Angela Klopstech, Margit Koemeda-Lutz, Rosaria Filoni and Barbara Lewis. If members are attracted to the themes in the abstracts, they are invited to translate the entire article for the native speakers in their societies who do not read English.

Besides the five articles, there is a poem by Linda Neal called, "Toward Water". She has written a short note about how writing poetry is like a good Bioenergetic session! Jacqueline Mills has written a book review of *Bend Into Shape: Techniques for Bioenergetic Therapists*. This new book was completed in 2011 and is a compilation of Bioenergetic interventions. It was written by Vincentia Schroeter and Barbara Thomson. The cover for this journal is a photo of a drawing by Vincentia that illustrates one of the techniques from this new book.

The editors would like to thank the reviewers and copy editors who turned a professional eye to the works included for this volume. Thanks go to Mae Nasciemento, Tarra Stariell, Peter Fernald, and Nirmala Bhat.

Enjoy reading this volume of the IIBA journal.

Sincerely,

Vincentia Schroeter
December 5, 2011

Neuroscience, Attachment and Love

Helen Resneck-Sannes

Abstracts

English

Findings from the neuroscientific research with its emphasis on attachment are presented. The focus of this research is primarily on the body in the brain and there is little interest or discussion of what goes on below the head. This neuroscientific view of attachment is contrasted with the attachment theories of Harry Harlow and Alexander Lowen, both based on the relationship between the mother and infant's bodies. Other forms of somatic therapies are compared with bioenergetics, pointing out a few of the ideas they have borrowed from the theory and practice of bioenergetics, but have not truly understood. Finally, I present a model of psychotherapeutic change based on the therapist's responses being shaped by the early attachment needs of the client, which reflect the underpinnings of love.

Key words: neuroscience, attachment, somatic psychotherapy, touch, love

Neurowissenschaft, Bindung und Liebe (German)

Ergebnisse aus der neurowissenschaftlichen Forschung mit Fokussierung auf Bindung werden vorgestellt. Der Fokus dieser Forschung richtet sich primär auf den Körper im Gehirn, mit wenig Interesse daran oder Diskussion dessen, was unterhalb des Kopfes geschieht. Diese neurowissenschaftliche Sicht von Bindung wird mit den Bindungstheorien von Harry Harlow und Alexander Lowen kontrastiert, die jeweils auf der Beziehung zwischen dem Köper der Mutter und dem des Kindes basieren. Andere Formen von somatischen Therapien werden mit der Bioenergetik verglichen. In diesem Zusammenhang wird auf einige Ideen hingewiesen, die aus der Theorie und Praxis der Bionergetischen Analyse geborgt, aber nicht wirklich verstanden sind. Abschließend wird ein Model von psychotherapeutischer Veränderung vorgestellt. Es basiert auf den Reaktionen des Therapeuten, als geformt von den frühen Bindungsbedürfnissen des Klienten, und reflektiert damit die Grundlagen von Liebe.

Schlüsselwörter: Neurowissenschaft, Bindung, Berührung, somatische Psychotherapien, Liebe

Neuroscience, Attachement et Amour (French)

Les découvertes qui sont présentées ici viennent de la recherche neuroscientifique avec l'importance qu'elle donne à l'attachement. Le "focus (centre)" de cette recherche est principalement "le corps dans le cerveau" et on y trouve peu d'intérêt ou de discussion sur ce qui se passe au-dessous de la tête. Cette vision neuroscientifique de l'attachement se trouve en contraste avec les théories de l'attachement de Harry Harlow et Alexander Lowen, toutes deux basées sur la relation entre les corps de la mère et de l'enfant. D'autres formes de thérapies somatiques sont comparées à la bioénergie, elles indiquent quelques unes des idées qu'elles ont empruntées à sa théorie et sa pratique mais elles ne les ont pas vraiment comprises. Finalement, je présente un modèle de changement psychothérapeutique basé sur les réponses du thérapeute qui seront formées par les besoins précoces d'attachement du client, qui reflète les "underpinnings" de l'amour.

Mots Clé: neuroscience, attachement, somatique psychotherapies, ecouter, amour

Neurociencia, Apego y Amor (Spanish)

Se presentan los hallazgos desde la investigación neurocientífica enfatizando el apego. El centro de esta investigación reside principalmente en el cerebro en el cuerpo y hay poco interés en discutir qué ocurre por debajo de la cabeza. Este enfoque neurocientífico del apego contrasta con las teorías del apego de Harry Harlow y Alexander Lowen ambas basadas en la relación entre los cuerpos de la madre y el bebé. Se comparan otros enfoques de terapias somáticas con la bioenergética, señalando algunas de las ideas que han tomado prestadas de la teoría y práctica del análisis bioenergético, sin comprenderlas profundamente. Finalmente, presento un modelo de cambio psicoterapéutico basado en como las respuestas del terapeuta son modeladas por las tempranas necesidades de apego del cliente, lo que refleja los apuntalamientos del amor.

Conceptos clave: neurociencia, apego, psicoterapia somática, contacto, amor

Neuroscienze, attaccamento e amore (Italian)

Vengono presentate delle scoperte che vengono dalla ricerca neuroscientifica, con particolare attenzione all'attaccamento. Il focus di questa ricerca riguarda il corpo nel cervello e c'è poco interesse o dibattito su ciò che accade al di sotto della testa. Questo punto di vista neuroscientifico sull'attaccamento è in contrasto con le teorie dell'attaccamento di Harry Harlow e di Alexander Lowen, entrambe basate sulla relazione tra i corpi delle madri e dei bambini. Altri tipi di terapie corporee sono paragonate alla bioenergetica, evidenziando alcune delle idee che hanno preso in prestito dalla teoria e dalla prassi bioenergetica senza comprenderle realmente. Infine, presento un modello di cambiamento terapeutico basato su risposte del terapeuta modellate sui bisogni primari di attaccamento dei pazienti, che riflettono i precursori dell'amore.

Parole chiave: Neuroscienze, attaccamento, psicoterapia corporea, contatto, amore

Neurociência, Apego e Amor (Portuguese)

São apresentadas descobertas da pesquisa em neurociência com ênfase no apego. O foco desta pesquisa é, primariamente, o corpo no cérebro e há pouco interesse ou discussão sobre o que acontece abaixo da cabeça. Esta visão neurocientífica do apego é comparada com as teorias do apego de Harry Harlow e Alexander Lowen, ambas baseadas na relação entre os corpos da mãe e do bebê. Outras formas de terapia somática são comparadas com a Bioenergética, enfatizando algumas idéias que elas tomaram emprestadas da teoria e prática da bioenergética, mas sem que se houvesse um verdadeiro entendimento a respeito destas.

Finalmente, apresento um modelo de mudança psicoterapêutica baseado nas respostas do terapeuta sendo formadas pelas necessidades precoces de apego do cliente, as quais refletem os fundamentos do amor.

Palavras-chave: Neurociência, apego, toque, psicoterapias somáticas, amor

Findings from the neuroscience research are discussed, primarily regarding the field of attachment, and it's emphasis on the body in the brain and I point out there is little interest or discussion of what goes on below the head. This neuroscientific view of attachment is in contrast to the attachment theories of Harry Harlow and Alexander Lowen, both based on the relationship between the mother and infant's bodies. Other forms of somatic therapies are compared with bioenergetics pointing out a few of the ideas they have borrowed from the theory and practice of bioenergetics, but have not truly understood. Finally, a model of psychotherapeutic change is presented based on the therapist's responses being shaped from the early attachment needs of the client, which reflect the underpinnings of love.

In this paper I risk being a fool by talking about love in the therapy relationship. However, I follow in the footsteps of two brave men before me, both who were renegades and creators – Al Lowen and Harry Harlow. They were very different people. Harlow was at the University of Wisconsin, Madison, when I was there, and he was a shy and retiring fellow. Most of us know that Lowen was aggressive and forceful, but both men challenged the zeitgeist of the psychological field during their times. Harlow emphasized the importance of physical contact for attachment and love. Lowen focused on the body and it's muscular holding patterns. Both men were convinced of the importance of the mother's body for early attachment experiences, for the creation of bonding, for the development of pathology; and for Harlow, love.

After rereading the current neuroscientific research again, I was struck by several things. The first is the importance of attachment. Alan Schore has written extensively on the importance of the baby's early experience with his or her primary caretakers for building and developing the infant's right brain. He and others have focused on the caretaker's ability to downregulate and provide appropriate stimulation to the infant. They have emphasized primarily eye-to-eye gaze and the mother's voice, prosody. However, one important ingredient is ignored, that so permeates the theory of attachment in the literature of bioenergetic analysis, and that is the physical contact between the caretaker and the child, which was emphasized by both Harry Harlow and Al Lowen. It is interesting to me that the neuroscience literature is complete with findings regarding attachment and downregulation and emotional integration; face-to-face and eye-to-eye contact; but there is little mention of holding and touch in the neuroscience literature. Instead, emphasis is placed on mind-to-mind interactions, and little importance is given to what happens below the head. This is in contrast to Harry Harlow's view of mothering, as described by Deborah Blum in her article, "The Inventor of the Cloth Mother". She says:

> "In the late 1950s, … Harry F. Harlow set himself a challenge: he would build a perfect mother for the baby monkeys in his laboratory. There were, of course, some practical challenges to perfection. The mothers had to stand up to the tendency of little monkeys to chew, unscrew, and take apart all objects in their cages. Harlow and his psychology students first tried making the heads out of inexpensive pine balls. The small animals gnawed those into pulp.
>
> 'Professor Harlow,' one of the students told him worriedly. 'The baby monkeys are destroying the mothers.' Harlow, typically, was amused. He lit another in his ceaseless chain of cigarettes and deadpanned his answer: 'Children have been destroying their parents for years.'
>
> The scientists switched to hard maple billiard balls for the heads. They used bicycle reflectors for the eyes, hard plastic for the curved mouth and jug-handle ears. In photographs, Harlow's lab-designed perfect mother has a face that seems half-clown, half-insect. But then, as he would later point out, 'a face that will stop a clock won't stop a baby.' It wasn't the head, or the bug-eyed face, that was the point of the experiment anyway. It was the body that mattered.

> The body of the ideal mother, Harlow believed, would be as soft as a cushion, warm as sunlight. Under his direction, the 'cloth mother' would have a cylindrical terry cloth body padded with fluffy filling and warmed by a light bulb. He was positive, even before the study was finished, that she would prove to the world that babies need a soft touch. An irrepressible writer of verse, he serenaded the cloth mother in a 1958 speech to his fellow psychologists: 'Though mother may be short on arms/Her skin is full of warmth and charms/and mother's touch on baby's skin/endears the heart that beats within'. Perhaps, there was something absolutely essential, in what Harlow called 'contact comfort.' Perhaps, he suggested, in those early days, touch is our most effective way to convey love" (Blum, D., The Inventor of the Cloth Mother, NZZFolio, 2003 (8)).

Then, Harlow began to study the dark side of love, or what happens when monkeys are left without physical contact. Monkeys that had a wire mother did not known how to bond with others in the community. They didn't know how to play, have sex, to care for their young. Monkeys left in a cage with another monkey, and I saw this, spent their time wrapped around each other in a fierce hug, striving for contact. And then, monkeys left totally alone, fell into a deep depression and died. One of my professors, Chuck Snowden, hated the cage that held the isolated monkeys so much that he called it "the pit of despair". And shortly after Harlow left, he tore it down.

I suppose you are beginning to wonder why I am so concerned about attachment at this point, as this information has been available for quite some time. My answer is personal, and I want to share it with you. David Campbell for many years has been reminding us of it's importance, and Bob Hilton in a talk in Portugal some years ago described his attachment to Al Lowen, like being one of those ducks that early on imprint to their caregiver asking: "Are you my mommy?" I lost one of my primary attachment figures, at four years of age. Her name was Helen Bell. In a previous paper, I wrote about my unconscious body or implicit memory of my experiences with her. I described how the morning after the birth of my own infant who, I was lucky to birth at home, I began dancing to Gospel music, without any conscious memory or knowing, until many years later when my aunt told me that Helen Bell had danced with me as an infant. And, as I have said, I lost her when I was four years old. Looking back, that was not an easy year in my life, as I had my tonsils removed with ether as an anesthetic. The problem with ether is that while the brain is asleep, the body experiences the pain, and it is encoded in a different part of consciousness, but not forgotten. I also fell off of a sliding board and was briefly unconscious, and then a month later I tripped on a step and hit my head and had to have stitches. I was not a particularly clumsy child, but was caught in some repetitive traumatic field, which we now have a clearer understanding about from the trauma literature. But what I couldn't remember, experience and grieve was the loss of Helen Bell. I was told that I was so attached to her, that once when our house caught fire, I calmly followed her out and would have gone anywhere with her. When David Campbell spoke on attachment and I told of him of my loss, he looked at me wisely, but still I really did not feel the loss. It wasn't until recently, when I read a book called, *The Help*, that I was flooded with memories of Helen Bell and was able to finally grieve and mourn my loss of her. I don't remember her eyes, although I still remember my mother's, whose eyes were a vibrant, sparkly blue green. But, I do remember the feel of Helen's breasts, the sound of her voice as she carried me, and the rich smell of her. Somehow, the book, like the birth of my daughter aroused those implicit stored memories of Helen Bell, memories of a real body, stored in my brain.

I will now tell you another story of a famous man, who suffered from early attachment loss. His story illustrates how our early attachment experiences impact our later adult choices. This is the story of Siddhartha or the Buddha. Queen Maya, Siddhartha's mother died 7 days after his birth. His father remarried and both his stepmother and father loved the young Siddhartha very much. He grew up amid the walls of the palace, living the life of the adored prince. When of age, he married a beautiful woman. It is written that he was so enraptured with her, that one day, while making love, they fell off a roof of the palace and continued without interruption. She gave birth to a son, but a few nights after his birth, Siddhartha looked at his perfect newborn son and his lovely wife, but refused to hold the infant, knowing that with that body to body bonding, he would become attached, and then be unable to leave. The story unfolds that Siddhartha left the palace, seeking enlightenment only to return many years later, realizing that Bodhisattva knowledge lies within. Knowing what we do now about mother/infant attachment and how those experiences are stored in the right brain, i.e. body memories, one wonders if Siddhartha's refusal to hold his own son and become attached was an unconscious avoidance of remembering the loss of his own mother. He looked, but he knew that once he held the infant, he would be attached and unable to leave.

We can gather from the story of Siddhartha and Harlow's research, the importance of physical contact and touch for infant and caretaking bonding and attachment. Although the neuroscience literature directs us to the importance of body to body bonding, the focus is primarily on managing arousal.

Listen closely to the following quote from one of my favorite books, *A General Theory of Love.*

> "Psychotherapy is physiology ... a somatic state of relatedness ... it alters the living brain. Mammals ... become attuned to one another's evocative signals and alter the structure of one another's nervous systems. Speech is a fancy neocortical skill, but therapy belongs to the older realm of the emotional mind, the limbic brain.
>
> These nonverbal communication channels are the language of the right hemisphere and literally wire up the child's early developing right hemisphere. They are the same circuits we utilize for 'rewiring' in the reparative attachment relationship called psychotherapy" (p. 168–169).

Two issues prevalent in the neuroscience literature are illustrated from the above quote. First, although the word somatic is used, it is the body in the brain, the mind that is still the focus of interest. Secondly, the neuroscience literature on attachment is focused primarily on the limbic system and the up regulation (excitation) and down regulation of the developing infant's nervous system by the caretaker. While discussing the ability of the therapist to regulate the client's nervous system, the specific developmental needs of the child at each age aren't considered. Little note is made of an ongoing process of adaptation and defensive reactions, as in the formation of character. Missing is the recurring tendency to think and feel as if we are still in the same environment in which we were born (i. e., character) and how we expect people to respond to us the same way our attachment figures treated us when we were growing up. It is as if as Bob Hilton has described, we have built a fortress to keep out the Indians from attacking us. They are gone now and we can't figure how to get out of the fortress. That fortress is our body, which operates at an unconscious level, so we aren't even aware of our assumptions. And it doesn't help that we find ourselves attracted to the same people, to whom we were attached when we were young. I do believe that as adults we become attached to one another without necessarily needing body-to-body contact, although it helps. However, infants sink into marasumus and die without physical contact. And most importantly for us as therapists, it is important to remember that the amount and quality of physical holding and relatedness we experienced in our infancy affects our emotional, as well as our physical development.

Since the idea of a body has now become important, other somatic psychotherapies are being developed. These other somatic modalities have taken ownership of many of the concepts of Bioenergetic Analysis (BA) without acknowledging their origin. And what is even more disconcerting, while using the language of BA, these other psychotherapies haven't truly understood some of the most important concepts of Bioenergetics and how they function, primarily those body interventions we so easily take for granted. George Downing's comments at Alexander Lowen's memorial in April, 2009, reminded me that: although we as a community have hopefully taken for granted the importance of body to mind resonance, i.e. the body/mind connection, *the other somatic schools of psychotherapy have adopted many of our techniques and ideas without understanding the literal ground on which we stand.*

Let us start with grounding. It is one of the most basic principles of bioenergetics and the word is used by so many other somatic modalities. It doesn't mean being centered or present, although these are both aspects of grounding. It doesn't mean necessarily going over into a bend over, although that is definitely helpful. I have had several clients who had previously been treated by Reichians, Radix, and Hakomi therapists, all who were excellent practitioners. Those clients, when I asked, all said that they knew how to ground. When I asked them to ground, none of them actually knew how. With the introduction of bioenergetic grounding, they sensed a change in how they handled being overwhelmed in their lives and began to feel a sense of self-possession. When one truly knows that she can stand up and feel supported by her own two feet without fear of falling backwards or forwards without bracing for the next attack, allowing the body to sink and rise with the energy of the earth. When one solidly feels held by oneself and the ground, then one truly begins to experience self-possession.

Now, if you choose, by following these simple instructions, you can have an opportunity to experience "grounding". First, stand up with your knees locked, your jaw tightly closed and stomach held in.

Look around the room at people and note quietly without speaking out loud, two words that describe how you feel. Now, stand with your legs about hip width apart. Let your mouth hang open and jaw relax. Inhale softly, bend your knees and exhale as you straighten without locking your knees. Again, remember to allow your mouth to hang open. Your eyes are also open but with a soft focus. Repeat bending your knees as you inhale, and straightening you legs on each exhale. Do this several times, and each time you straighten, push your feet into the floor, like you are at the beach, and are trying to sink into the center of the earth. Now, look around the room and see how you feel. Use two words to describe it. This is such a simple concept, but a very complex series of events.

When you bend and straighten your legs, you are actually charging the body, but sending the charge down, rather than into your head. Such an exercise not only calms you, but it also builds the relaxing GABA fibers of the mind. Gaba Amino Buteric Acid, are thin inhibitory tracks that run from the brain centers behind your forehead, to the lower ones. These fibers reduce the chatter in your limbic brain. (Valium and other sedative-like drugs work because they activate these GABA pathways).

Let us look at some other somatic psychotherapies. Hakomi took bioenergetic character types without really understanding the developmental holding patterns in the body. Lowen meant character to be embedded in the body. Hakomi has added a very powerful method to the practice of psychotherapy, the concept of mindfulness.

This is a useful addition as people tend to get stuck in negative thought/arousal patterns. Mindfulness enables one to observe these patterns without becoming activated. However, Hakomi does not directly assess the developmental holding patterns, nor does it have the powerful somatic interventions developed in Bioenergetic Analysis.

Also, I am an advocate of Somatic Experiencing, which was developed by Peter Levine. No other theory has provided as complete analysis of the neurological and biological effects of trauma. The powerful and effective somatic interventions that have arisen from Peter Levine's extensive exploration into the origins and effects of trauma have impacted the entire field of psychology's treatment of PTSD. I also think that Family Systems Theory, Richard Schwartz and his use of what he calls, "protectors" has changed the way I now treat defensive maneuvers by the client. However, neither Somatic Experiencing nor Family Systems Theory is relational. Those mind to mind/body to body, transferential/counter-transferential interactions, which are so integral to the process of psychotherapy are ignored in these systems.

Any intervention must not only be based on the client's level of development when the trauma occurred, but also the contact (whether it involves voice, eye gaze, or touch) must be contingently responsive. Contingently responsive means the contact should vary in response to the infant or client's reaction. Touch should be hard or soft, fast or slow and voice should be high or low, soft or loud, depending on whether the client or baby finds it pleasant.

A friend from graduate school, Ron Slaby and his associates carried out a remarkable study. (Roedell, & Slaby 1977). They took a group of 6-month old babies and provided them with walkers. Then they presented the babies with three different attachment figures. The first attachment figures touched the babies, rocked and patted them but weren't responsive, neither talking to nor looking at the infants. These persons were more like what we would call a disassociated caretaker or as Andre Green calls it: "the dead mother". The second attachment figures didn't touch the babies but were distally responsive in vocalization and eye gaze, i.e. looking and smiling at the infants. The behaviors of these attachment figures were contingent on the babies' responses, sustaining mutual eye contact, smiling, and breaking gaze when the infant looked away. Babies break eye contact when it feels too stimulating. The third figures neither touched nor were they distally responsive to the infants. Of course the babies chose to approach the responsive attachment figures. Touch alone is not enough. We need to provide the response that the client needs at that time. Character analysis and bodily holding patterns are guides to what happened to the client during those early interactions. If clients are touch or gaze avoidant, we can hypothesize that their caretakers weren't responding with sensitivity to their needs for soothing or excitation vis a vis eye contact or physical contact during infancy.

I am emphasizing two issues, both of which can guide the therapist toward being able to provide the best response to the client at that time. First, as therapists our interventions should be governed both by the client's reactions to us, that is contingently responsive. And secondly, bioenergetic holding patterns can guide us into making a diagnosis of the client's level of development at the time of the issue, which they are currently confronting. Such understanding enables the therapist to modify her interventions contingent upon the client's response. I will now give you an example, which emphasizes the importance of a developmental diagnosis, for understanding the client's reaction. For the purpose of this paper l call the client, Ingrid. Personal details, although interesting, are not important for the point I wish to make here. She had been working with several other somatic therapies, i.e. Richard Schwartz, Family Systems therapy, emotional processing, and others, which had left her over-activated and highly aroused. I began to work with her slowly, trying to enable her to feel her legs and the ground. She wanted to continue with more somatic work to aid in her downregulation, so I sent her to a practitioner of Somatic Experiencing. There was an incident in which a prowler had broken into her house when she was young and fondled her, and that therapist began working with the trauma from an inescapable attack. She saw her going into a calm quiet place as a resource. What I saw (and I knew from her history) was an oral/schizoid collapse. Her shoulders slumped forward; her eyes weren't blank in shock, but not contactful. It was as if the world was devoid of soothing objects, and all she could do was give up and withdraw into a state, which the client described as a place of deep exhaustion. This is the state of the infant who goes into a collapse to self soothe, when there is no attuned caretaker. These other somatic therapies don't have the deep understanding that has been developed in the theory and practice of BA of the correlation between the first three years of life, the client's experience with her caretaker, and the body that develops. An important part of trauma work is developing a resource, a place to return again and again when the nervous system is overwhelmed. However, if one is not trained in reading different holding patterns and knowing the resources that one is capable of during different developmental stages, what may look like a resource is actually a character defense. In this situation the therapist needs to be present for the client, and aware of the deep helplessness, which is felt by the client. What the trauma therapist might label as a response to an "inescapable attack" was the result of an earlier character issue, in which withdrawal into self-soothing is Ingrid's recurring defensive response to stress, rather than only a response to the trauma of the attack. To me working with the body without being able to see and notice holding patterns is like being invited into an art gallery where one can feel the paintings, but not truly see them.

I also challenge another theorem from the trauma literature, that not much trauma still remains if the client can give a coherent narrative of his history. Fundamental to Van der Kolk and his collaborators' work is the assumption that psychological health is bound up with an individual's ability to provide a coherent temporal narrative of a traumatic experience (Van der Kolk & Van der Hart 1995; Van der Kolk 1996). One of my client's, whom I will call Frank, repeatedly describes two key events from his life, in which he didn't follow the calling of his internal voice, but instead succumbed to his mother's desires of what she thought was best for him. He tells of these events repeatedly, without much feeling. However, as Frank is speaking, I notice his chest tightens, and his shoulders pull forward, disconnecting his arms from the rest of his body. Although he doesn't look like he is in a high state of arousal; on the contrary, he is disassociated from his body, cutting off his emotional reaction and feeling very little. I point out his body's position and have him exaggerate and release it. Once again, I have him tell me his story, and this time, Frank's anger and grief emerge regarding those decisions. As he reconnects to the emotions behind these decisions, I am able to direct his attention to how he cuts himself off from his feelings, and from using his arms to both protect himself and from reaching out to get his needs met. So, what looks like a coherent narrative is really a story, disassociated from feeling.[1]

Based on the animal literature, there is some powerful evidence that it is the bodily/emotional responses that are the important part of the therapeutic process, not the story. This recent research supports the concept that it is the emotional responses that are evoked separate from the intellectual and cognitive responses from therapy as usual, that are important for change in the therapeutic process. It has been found, more recently that even when investigators surgically eliminate all the neo-cortex areas of the brain, the area of cognitions in experimental animals, they still grow up to be seemingly normal creatures as far as their basic set of emotional energies are concerned. "What this research implies is that we can work more directly

1 Main describes securely attached parents as rated by the Adult Attachment Interview (Main 2000) as being able to revisit highly evocative terrain of their attachment histories, recalling very troubling experiences with their parents and still being able to maintain a balanced perspective. Although Frank appears to be able to do this, the only way to be clear about how Frank maps onto attachment researcher's classification of coherence would be to have them rate him in an Adult Attachment Interview. And Robert Lewis suggests that: Your description of your patient and what ensued from your intervention is internally consistent and obviously accurate – except, as I've said, I don't know if attachment researchers would describe his narrative as coherent. The proof of the coherence as a predictor of health hypothesis would seem to that the way they code the responses to the AAI questions has been consistently and powerfully predictive (70–80%) both of parenting behavior and how the offspring of these parents respond at one year to the Strange Situation test. I think a child's attachment classification also predicts the type of narrative he/she later develops as an adult. So it is hard to argue with this kind of data. What interests me is that there are probably all kinds of facial expressions, vocal timbres, gestures and things going on below the interviewees' necks that are-out of awareness-going into the AAI assessments! (Lewis, R., 2011).

with emotional feelings through body dynamics than cognitive inputs" (Panskepp, J., 2009, p. 19).

I have been talking about emotions, but in my introduction I promised I would talk about love and there hasn't even been a hint of that feeling in this paper so far. So, now I will introduce the topic by once more quoting from Harry Harlow. This is an excerpt from Harlow's speech to the American Psychological Association in 1958.

> "The apparent repression of love by modem psychologists stands in sharp contrast with the attitude taken by many famous and normal people. The word 'love' has the highest reference frequency of any word cited in Bartlett's book of *Familiar Quotations.* It would appear that this emotion has long had a vast interest and fascination for human beings, regardless of the attitude taken by psychologists; but the quotations cited, even by famous and normal people, have a mundane redundancy. These authors and authorities have stolen love from the child and infant and made it the exclusive property of the adolescent and adult."

For instance, we have the excellent paper by David Finlay on intimacy and love published post mortem in the journal, but that is about mature bonding between adults.

In contrast, Harlow goes on to say:

> "Thoughtful men, and probably all women, have speculated on the nature of love. From the developmental point of view, the general plan is quite clear: The initial love responses of the human being are those made by the infant to the mother or some mother surrogate. From this intimate attachment of the child to the mother, multiple learned and generalized affectional responses are formed" (Harlow 2000, p. 573–685).

Our adult capacity to love is formed out of our early attachment feelings to the persons who we loved and who probably loved us the most. However, these early experiences are also filled with unmet longings, traumatic encounters, abandonment, and sometimes terror. I remember lying on the mat, after my therapist had worked diligently for many sessions on opening my heart. As, I lay there crying, she asked, "Aren't you happy to be feeling your love, now?" When I entered bioenergetic analysis, I was hoping to open up to my feelings, but naively I had thought I would only experience more joy, love, and passion in my life. At the time of this therapy session, my mother was dying from a rare form of leukemia, and

I was feeling terrible grief at losing her. Also, my truth was that the people who loved me the most, my family, also had hurt me the most deeply. So, when we open ourselves and our clients to those emotions from our early attachment years, we are inviting ourselves to experience some difficult feelings. I remind us now of Winnicott's paradoxical connotation, the fear of breakdown is the fear of a breakdown that has already happened but not been suffered (Winnicott, 1963). For healing, the injury often needs to be suffered in the therapy room, within and between the client and therapist.

> "An irony of the therapeutic process (and one unpopular with patients) is that successful therapy ... cannot escape reliving the emotional experiences he most wishes to rid himself of. If we could hone psychotherapy to an instrument of inconceivable precision, it would still entail instances of traumatic repetition. The only guarantee against them is an emotional distance that dooms limbic effectiveness" (Lewis,T., Amini F., and Lannon, R., 2000, p. 186).

By love in the therapy room I am not referring to the mother's love for her infant. As Frank Lachmann (1994) points out, clients are not babies or toddlers, who need us to mother them. Babies differ from pathological adults. Pathology develops in an individual who has been experiencing the world longer than the infant. The adult has many more capacities than the infant, even though the adult's body has erected defenses against experiencing the early traumas of the infant and child.

I will now give a final example from my Bioenergetic practice, which hopefully will illustrate this principle and why I bring up the notion of love in the therapy room. It also illustrates why only following a client's self report about his or her body, which is the hallmark of interventions from almost all other somatic therapies, is not enough. One of my clients, whom I will call, Tom described a "dead area" in his body, just above his navel, which I could see was an area of tension and deep holding. Departing from our more usual way of processing material, I invited him over the stool. As Tom sent his breath to the "dead area", he began to experience a great deal of early sadness and grief. In the past he was caught between his need of wanting me close and his fear of having to give up himself for the contact. I am feeling his sadness and say to him: "It is alright to feel and cry. I am here." He has enough presence to reach out and grab my hand, which he has never done before and says to me several times again and again, that my words are important. Once more, I tell him that I am here with him, that it is ok to feel what he feels; he doesn't have to be strong. Now, I am really feeling his sadness and with tears in my eyes, I ask him to look at me and I repeat again the words: "I am here and it is okay to have your feelings." He breaks down sobbing and leans on me.

It is my physical, emotional presence, along with knowing the right words to say to my client at that moment that are so important. I know the right words, because we have worked together for over a year. Tom's father was an angry and sometimes violent drunk, who terrified my client, so much that he slept with his bedroom door locked. His mother left him at four months of age for a week's vacation. He recalled that later, when he was older, he felt he could receive her love, as long as he was a super achieving straight "A" student. The stool opens him up to his vulnerable feelings, and I know from working with him how important it is that I am there with him. In case I am not clear, I want to strongly state that it isn't the technique of the breathing stool that heals. I agree with this quote by Daniel Stern, which is echoed in the writings of Allan Schore:

> "Most of us have been dragged kicking and screaming to the realization that what really works in psychotherapy is the relationship between therapist and client. We are all devastated by this reality because we spent years and a lot of money learning a particular technique or theory, and it is very disheartening to realize that what we learned is only the vehicle or springboard to create a relationship; which is where the work happens" (Stern, D., 2008).

Knowing the body is not enough, although it helps us know where to intervene with clients and how. Although it is important to be able to read a client's early attachment issues from the holding patterns and muscular development of their body, it is not sufficient. Nor is it the cathartic emotional response from releasing the area held in a "dead spot" for this client, or an area of contraction enough. The fear of breakdown is the fear of a breakdown that has already happened but not been suffered (Winnicott, 1963). The injury needs to be suffered in the therapy room, within the client and between the client and therapist. I had to suffer the breakdown with Tom. Whether I cried or not, I had a body resonance out of my strong feelings of caring and connection to this man. That connection didn't happen immediately. It was developed after many hours of interactions, in which each of us allowed ourselves to soften into knowing the other. I can honestly say that I truly love Tom. When he was shaking and vulnerable over that stool, I wanted to gather him up in my arms and soothe him. Instead, I resonated with his pain and gave him permission to come back to a real and earlier self, who he had so long ago left behind. Now he could have his feelings of grief for what he had lost, as there was another person to grieve with him.

Ed Tronick says that certain events are critical for pivotal changes in the dyadic consciousness of the therapist and client. I would like to add in the dyadic body/emotional/consciousness. For a session to function as a pivotal point of change, Tronick says the therapy session must contain the following elements:

1. It is marked by a sense of departure from the habitual way of proceeding in the therapy. It is a novel happening that the ongoing framework can neither account for nor encompass. It is the opposite of business as usual.
2. It is neither sustained nor fulfilled by a technical response.
3. It is not a transference interpretation.
4. It is dealing with what is happening here and now between us. The response of the therapist is both spontaneous and affective.
5. It is happening here and now and can't be verbally explicated.

I repeat that although Tronick describes it as a dyadic state of consciousness, I feel it is a dyadic state of body/emotional/consciousness. I didn't make an interpretation or explain to the client that he was crying because his mother had abandoned him unless he met her requirements of her image of him. Instead, I was there to experience with him the pain of that abandonment. I had tears in my eyes, and my heart ached for what had happened to him and he felt it. I loved him.

Working with clients week after week, sometimes meeting several times during a week is such an intimate experience, that I find that I am unable to prevent myself from caring for them. Only with a few close friends and family do I share such an intimate connection that I have with my clients. Of course the relationship is one-sided in that their story and feelings are the primary focus, but that does not prevent me from loving them. In case you might misunderstand what I am saying I want to point out that, even though I love Tom, all of my reactions aren't supportive. Out of a fear of abandonment, he had become a helpless victim in the relationship with his wife and male peers, who were taking advantage of him. My attachment to Tom opened up my heart and I was frustrated that I couldn't protect him. In fact, at one point I had sadistic feelings, because he wouldn't stand up for himself with his wife and colleagues. Also, during our therapy sessions he was willing to blindly follow what I said, without thinking or hesitation, or checking in with what he really felt. I was frustrated so I developed a Simple Simon exercise, in which I led him into positions that he couldn't possibly follow, and that made him look foolish. I was aware at the time that he would feel humiliated. That session was also a very powerful session, and we had to work it through many times. However, I believe that it came out of feelings of attachment and love for him and was a pivotal session for change, both in the therapy and in his relationship with his wife and peers.

Therapy is such an intimate relationship. Clients come to us and eventually reveal their most hurt and vulnerable selves. I want to share this quote from the philosopher, Shopenhauer. I actually came across it in a book, authored by Irving Yalom:

> "We should treat with indulgence every human folly, failing, and vice bearing in mind that what we have before us are simply our own failings, follies, and vices. For they are just the failings of mankind to which we also belong and accordingly we all have the same failings buried within ourselves. We should not be indignant with others for these vices simply because they do not appear in us at the moment" (Yalom, I., 2005, p. 323).

I think with me, it is a little different. I love my clients because they have my vices or shortcomings. For as Rainer Maria Rilke states: "Love consists in this, that two solitudes protect and touch and greet each other." I may not have shared my clients' life experiences, but I can certainly resonate with their emotional reactions. When I do not judge their failings, I feel kinder toward my own. Their joys and sorrows open my heart to them and to myself, despite my own failings, defenses, and "dead spots". So I will end with this quote from Zora Neale Hurston, which I think summarizes much of what I have been saying. "Love makes your soul crawl out from its hiding place."

References

Blum, D. (2003): The Inventor of the Cloth Mother, NZZFolio (8).

Green, André (2001): The dead mother. In his Life narcissism/death narcissism (Andrew Weller, Trans.). London, New York: Free Associations Books.

Harlow, H. (1958): "The Nature of Love", [1], University of Wisconsin, First published in American Psychologist, 13, 673–685, Posted March 2000.

Lachmann, F. (1994): Some contributions of empirical infant research to adult psychoanalysis: What have we learned? How can we apply it? Psychoanalytic Dialogues, 11(2), 167–187.

Lewis, T., Amini F., and Lannon, R. (2000): A General Theory of Love. New York: Random House.

Lewis, R. (2011): Personal communication.

Lowen, A. (1958): The Language of the Body. New York: Grune & Stratton, Inc.

Lowen, A. (1975): Bioenergetics. New York: Penguin Books.

Main, M. (2000): The organized categories of infant, child, and adult attachment: Flexible vs. inflexible attention under attachment-related stress. Journal of the American Psychoanalytic Association, 48 (4), 1055–1096.

Panskepp, J. (2009): "Brain emotional systems and qualities of mental life: From animal models of affect to implications for psychotherapeutics". In The Healing Power of Emotion, in Fosha, D. Siegel, D. and Solomon, M. (eds.) New York: WW. Norton & Co., Inc.

Resneck-Sannes, H. (2007): The Embodied Mind, in Bioenergetic Analysis, Vol. 17, 2007 pp. 39–56.

Roedell, W.C., & Slaby, R.G. (1977): The role of distal and proximal interaction in infant social preference formation. Developmental Psychology, 13, 266–273.

Schore, A. (1994): Affect Regulation and the Origin of the Self: The neurobiology of emotional development. New Jersey: Lawrence Erlbaum Associates, Inc.

Schore, A. (2003a): Affect Regulation and the Disorders of the Self. New York: W.W. Norton.

Schore, A. (2003b): Affect Dysregulation and Repair of the Self. New York: W.W. Norton.

Stern, D. (1985): The Interpersonal World of the Infant. New York: Basic Books.

Stern, D. (2008): Infant mental health Journal.

Tronick, E. (2007): The neurobehavioral and Social-Emotional Development of Infants and Children New York: W.W. Norton & Co.

Van der Kolk, B.A. (1996): Trauma and Memory. In B.A. van der Kolk, A.C. McFarlane, & L. Weisaeth (Eds.), Traumatic Stress: The Effects of Overwhelming Experience on Mind, Body, and Society (pp. 279–302). London: The Guilford Press.

Van der Kolk, B.A. & Van der Hart, O. (1995): The Intrusive Past: The Flexibility of Memory and the Engraving of Trauma. In C. Caruth (Ed.), Trauma: Explorations in Memory (pp. 158–82). Baltimore: The Johns HopkinsUniversity Press.

Winnicott, D.W. (1989): The fear of breakdown. In C. Winnicott, R. Shepherd, & M. Davis (Eds.), "Psycho-analytic explorations" (pp. 87–95). Cambridge, MA: Harvard University Press (Original work published 1963).

Winnicott, D. W. (1963): Dependence in infant care, child care, psychoanalytic setting. Int. J. Psychoanalysis., 44: 339–344.

Yalom, I (2005): The Schopenhauer Cure, New York: HarperCollins.

About the Author

Helen Resneck-Sannes, PhD, is a licensed psychologist, practicing psychotherapy in Santa Cruz, California for over thirty years. She is on the international faculty of the IIBA, and has taught in many countries around the world. Her numerous writings have been pioneering in integrating Bioenergetics with modern analytic, developmental, attachment, neuroscientific and trauma models in psychotherapy, and her articles have appeared in various psychological journals and books. Website: helenresneck.com.

An Object Relations Perspective on Bioenergetics and Pre-Oedipal Transferences

Garry Cockburn

Abstracts

English

Alexander Lowen's views on oedipal transference were formed within the intellectual framework of Freudian and Reichian drive theory and ego psychology. Lowen did not favor analytic work with transference and believed that countertransference indicated that the therapy was "faulted". This article critically examines his classical approach and offers a re-examination of pre-oedipal transference phenomena in a way that both honors Lowen's unique insights into the transformative power of Bioenergetic Analysis, and at the same time offers a Kleinian/Bionian object relations understanding of pre-oedipal transference that can be incorporated into modern Bioenergetic Analysis. An extended case example illustrates the effective integration of object relations theory and bioenergetic practice. The concluding discussion provides a rationale for introducing an object relations approach into Bioenergetic Analysis.

Key words: transference, countertransference, projective identification, paranoid-schizoid and depressive positions

Eine Objekt-Beziehungstheoretische Perspektive zur Bioenergetischen Analyse und zu prä-ödipalen Übertragungen (German)

Alexander Lowens Sichtweise von ödipaler Übertragung entwickelte sich im intellektuellen Rahmen der Freudschen und Reichianischen Triebtheorie und Ich-Psychologie. Lowen legte wenig Wert auf analytische Arbeit an Übertragung und sah Gegenübertragung als eine Indikation für "fehlerhafte" Therapie an. Der vorliegende Artikel setzt sich mit diesem klassischen Ansatz kritisch auseinander und bietet eine Re-Examinierung des Phänomens der praeödipalen Übertragung an. Unter Berücksichtigung von Lowens Einsichten in die transformative Kraft der Bioenergetischen Anayse wird ein Verständnis von präödipaler Übertragung aus Objekt-Beziehungstheoretischer Sicht vorgestellt, das in moderne Bioenergetische Analyse integriert werden kann. Die effektive Nutzung von Objekt-Beziehungstheorie und bioenergetischer Praxis wird in einem ausführlichen Fallbeispiel demonstriert.

Schlüsselwörter: Übertragung, Gegenübertragung, Projektive Identifikation, Paranoid-Schizoide und depressive Positionen

Une perspective des relations d'objet sur la bioenergie et les transferts pre-oedipiens (French)

Les pensées (opinions) d'Alexandre Lowen sur les transferts oedipiens se sont formées à l'intérieur du cadre intellectuel de la théorie de la pulsion et de la psychologie du moi de Freud et Reich. Lowen n'approuvait pas le travail analytique avec le transfert et il croyait que les contre-transferts indiquaient que la thérapie était "défectueuse". Cet article examine d'un point de vue critique son approche classique et offre une nouvelle étude du phénomène de transfert pré-oedipien qui, à la fois, honore la perspicacité exceptionnelle de Lowen dans le pouvoir de transformation de l'Analyse Bioénergétique et, en même temps, offre une compréhension en termes de relations d'objet des transferts pré-oedipiens qui peut être incorporée dans la bioénergie moderne. L'exemple d'un cas de grande ampleur illustre l'utilisation efficace de la théorie des relations d'objet et de la pratique bioénergétique.

Mots Clés: Transfert, Contre-transfert, Identification Projective, Positions Schizoïde-Paranoïde et Position Dépressive

Una perspectiva de las relaciones de objeto en el análisis bioenergético y las transferencias pre-edípicas (Spanish)

Las opiniones de Alexander Lowen con relación a la transferencia edípica se formaron en el marco intelectual de la Teoría de los Impulsos y la Psicología del Ego de Freud y Reich. Lowen no apoyó el trabajo analítico con las transferencias y creía que las contra transferencias indicaban que la terapia era "defectuosa". Este artículo examina críticamente su enfoque clásico y ofrece un re-examen del fenómeno de la transferencia pre-edípica de un modo que a la vez honra la comprensión única de Lowen acerca del poder transformador del análisis bioenergético, y al mismo tiempo ofrece una comprensión de las relaciones de objeto en las transferencias pre-edípicas que puede ser incorporada al análisis bioenergético moderno. El ejemplo de un caso ilustra el uso efectivo de la teoría de las relaciones de objeto y la práctica bioenergética.

Conceptos clave: Transferencia, Contra transferencia, Identificación proyectiva, Posiciones paranoide, esquizoide y depresiva

Una prospettiva sulla bioenergetica e i transfert pre-edipici basata sulle relazioni oggettuali (Italian)

Il punto di vista di A. Lowen sul transfert edipico si era formata all'interno della cornice della teoria degli istinti e della psicologia dell'Io freudiana e reichiana. Lowen non era a favore di un lavoro analitico con il transfert e credeva che il controtransfert indicasse che ci fossero problemi nella terapia. Questo articolo esamina criticamente il suo approccio classico e offre un riesame dei fenomeni del transfert pre-edipico per onorare la grande intuizione di Lowen sul potere trasformativo dell'analisi bioenergetica, e al tempo stesso offrire una comprensione legata alle relazioni oggettuali del transfert pre-edipico che può essere integrata nella bioenergetica moderna. Un caso clinico illustra la possibilità effettiva di utilizzare la teoria delle relazioni oggettuali e l'analisi bioenergetica.

Parole chiave: transfert, controtransfert, identificazione proiettiva, posizioni schizo-paranoide e depressiva

Uma perspectiva de relações objetais em Bioenergética e transferência pré-edípica (Portuguese)

A visão de Alexander Lowen da transferência edípica tinha como referência a teoria do drive e a psicologia do ego de Freud e Reich. Lowen não adotava o trabalho analítico com transferência e acreditava que a contratransferência indicava uma "falha" na terapia. Este artigo examina criticamente sua abordagem clássica e oferece uma reavaliação dos fenômenos de transferência pré-edípica, de modo tanto a honrar os "insights" únicos de Lowen referentes ao poder transformador da Análise Bioenergética, como a oferecer uma compreensão das relações de objeto da transferência pré-edípica que podem ser incorporados à moderna Bioenergética. Um estudo de caso ilustra o uso eficaz da teoria de relações de objeto e da prática bioenergética.

Palavras-chave: transferência, contra-transferência, identificação projetiva, posições esquizo-paranóide e depressiva

Introduction

In this paper[1] I would like to present some ideas on introducing object relations theory into Bioenergetic Analysis, with a particular focus on preoedipal transference and countertransference. Alexander Lowen's ideas on oedipal transference were developed within the intellectual framework of classical psychoanalytic and Reichian drive theory and ego psychology. He did not have readily available to him all of the developed intellectual resources we have today, e.g. object relations theory, self psychology, attachment theory, neuropsychology and affect regulation, etc. He chose, for a variety of reasons, the most powerful paradigm available to him in

1 A draft of this paper was presented at the Professional Development Workshop (PDW), Mt. Madonna, California, in October 2010. I would like to thank Elaine Tuccillo Ph.D. for her encouragement to develop the paper for publication and for her editorial assistance.

the 1950's and 1960's, namely Freudian ego psychology and drive theory, to elucidate his understanding of the transference and countertransference phenomena.

For the past several years I have been trying to understand the transference phenomena that I meet in the therapy room, both from a bioenergetic perspective and from an intersubjective psychoanalytic perspective using the Kleinian/Bionian line of object relations theory.

This paper will give a brief overview of Lowen's approach to transference. It will present a number of vignettes of the transference phenomena and provide an understanding of these phenomena, which both honors Lowen's deepest insights, and attempts to integrate one particular theoretical view of object relations into bioenergetics. This integration is illustrated with a case example, which is then followed by a discussion of a rationale for introducing an object relations perspective to Bioenergetic Analysis when considering pre-oedipal transferences.

Alexander Lowen and Transference

Lowen, in the first chapter of the *Language of the Body* (1971, p. 6f.) refers to the importance that Freud gave to the facts of transference and resistance in the therapeutic process. Lowen believed that neurotic (oedipal) transference and resistance were based on Freudian drive theory and that the suppression of sexual desires and fears are responsible for the transference projection onto the therapist (Lowen, 1971, pp. 8, 133).

Further to this, Lowen's intuitive focus on Ferenczi's "active method" lead him to value the approach he, Lowen, called "analysis from below". His elaboration of "analysis from below", showed how to go beneath the Freudian ego defences, (and hence, below neurotic transferences) and even beneath Reichian character analysis, and how to release the *"great wells of feeling which lie at the core of human beings"*, by working on energy processes at the somatic level. (1971, p. 13).

Guy Tonella (2008, p. 34; 2011, p. 65), in his ESMER[2] model, has shown how it was Lowen who established the link between the energetic and sen-

2 "ESMER" stands for **E**nergy, **S**ensory, **M**otor, **E**motional and **R**epresentation. These are the sequential developmental functions of the Self. Tonella has shown how Lowen, Piaget, Reich and Freud were the theorists who delineated the connections between each of these functional layers.

sory functions in the early development of the Self. Tonella's insights and ability to place Lowen within a broad paradigm of the development of the Self are most helpful in developing a newer bioenergetic understanding of pre-oedipal transference and countertransference.

Lowen outlined the potential of bioenergetic techniques to give rise to positive and negative transference and countertransference phenomena, even more powerfully than psychoanalytic techniques could do (1971, pp. xiii, 133). Lowen himself did "not favor verbal analysis", preferring to work directly with the energy of the body (2004, p. 243). And while he believed that transference issues could be worked through in therapy, he believed that countertransferential issues indicated that the therapist and the therapy were "faulted" (1995, p. 3). The therapist's countertransference "*reflects his involvement with his own ego image and his denial of the truth of the body … it will constitute an obstacle to the patient's recovery*" (1967, p. 251). This view of Lowen's was fully in accord with the many writers in the ego psychology tradition[3] who believed that countertransferential issues needed to be dealt with in one's own self-analysis (Brown, 2011, p. 33).

Lowen viewed the client's transference towards the therapist as the best way to delineate the patient's character structure (1971, p. 133f.). He did not, however, see countertransference as part of an intersubjective reality that could be used to understand the patient's inner world and enhance the therapy. He himself seemed easily able to handle transferential issues at the level of neurotic transference in his work with patients with oedipal character structures. But at the pre-oedipal level, where transference reflects early developmental and attachment issues, and more primitive relational dynamics and defenses, Lowen did not seem available for the type of intersubjective transference that Grotstein (2009, Vol.1, p. 225) calls "*projective (trans-)identification as a means of communication between infant/analysand and the mother/analyst*". We know this from the writings of Robert Hilton (2008, p. 9) and Robert Lewis (2007, p. 146), both of whom had pre-oedipal issues arising in their personal therapy with Lowen. He saw their bodies,

3 For an historical overview of the negative and positive views of countertransference within Psycho-analysis, read Slakter (1987, pp. 7–39). Annie Reich (1951), in a classic statement, viewed countertransference as "*the interference of the analyst's own unconscious needs and conflicts on his understandings or technique*". It was Paula Heimann (1950) who positively linked transference and countertransference, which is partially "*the patient's creation*" in the therapist.

but he failed to see "them". Interestingly, Lowen himself had written how Reich failed see him at this level and how he felt "doomed" (1975, p. 21). I have written elsewhere about the impact of this on the development of bioenergetics:

> "By rising above the *helplessness* of the baby, Lowen took a profound strategic stance that affects us today ... it also moved bioenergetics away from the earliest experiences of body and self in relationship, and away from the primary ground where 'oneself also includes the other'" (2008a, p. 18).

Vignettes

I would like to present several vignettes of transference and countertransference phenomena from my own practice, and for which I have found little guidance in Lowen's writings to understand them. I will then discuss my theoretical understanding of what might be happening.

1. A patient told me that my face was melting like plastic and changing into a face she did not recognize. We both entered into a trance-like fixed, staring gaze in which time and space appeared to stop still into a present moment that could have gone on forever, until I shook myself out of it and asked her what she was experiencing.
2. I started to feel very sleepy with a male patient, and could hardly stay awake over a period of 20 minutes, despite biting the inside of my cheek, pushing my thumb-nail into my hand till it hurt, and moving around in my chair. My tiredness did not seem to be related to the content matter the patient was talking about. Finally I said to him, "No doubt you aware I am feeling sleepy. Would you mind saying to me, Wake-up!" A shocked look came over his face, and he later reported that at that moment he had a visual hallucination of me changing into his father. The patient's mother was schizophrenic and the father had "never woken up" to the fact that she was a danger to the children from the moment they were born.
3. A male patient, whom a previous counsellor would only see if she had a security guard in the room with her, went into a kind of trance, rolled his eyes back into his head, clutched his heart, saying, "oh the pain, the pain!" and then was subject to violent shaking. He later reported that he had left his body and had run the gauntlet of evil entities who

were trying to pluck his heart from his body. One day he reported that there were two archangels in the room, one with a flaming sword and one with a book, to help reclaim his heart from the evil entities. As he clung onto me in terror and reached into the maw of hell to retrieve his heart, there was a very unusual tornado-type wind just outside my window. Later my wife asked me if I had felt the strange wind that hit the building. I had frequently felt on the edge of terror that I could be destroyed by incarnate evil when working with this man, but also had a conviction that I would be safe.

4. A woman priest, who had done 15 years psychoanalytic and Jungian therapy, and had come to me for bioenergetics, explained to me that she felt like she was trapped inside the Garden of Eden and that an angel with the flaming sword was preventing her from leaving. I felt an unbearable grief in the bottom of my soul, even though she did not look or sound sad. Three months later, she told me she felt like the words in Psalm 22, "They have *numbered* all my bones. *And* they have *looked and stared upon me. … with wonder on one so wretched, so crushed, so* broken."

Towards a Bioenergetic Object Relations Understanding of Pre-Oedipal Transference

How do we explain these phenomena? I believe it is possible to view the transferences/countertransferences in the above vignettes either:

a) through the lens of classical psychoanalysis and Lowenian bioenergetics, and see them as oedipal transferences that have been pushed regressively back into infancy, e.g. into the oral stage; or
b) see them as pre-oedipal transferences belonging to the earliest energetic and sensory levels of infancy, and reflecting relational experiences between the infant and their parent.

Bioenergetic therapists are trained to attune and resonate with the deepest core energetic and somatic elements. I think that what is needed to adequately do this is an intersubjective theoretical model, which is an advance on Lowenian drive theory, and which can help us understand transference phenomena at the pre-oedipal level. Robert Hilton (2008) has done this using the resources of the British Independents, Winnicott and Guntrip, to elaborate his "Relational Somatic Therapy"; Robert Lewis has done this using the resources of Attachment Theory and Neuroscience, and in his original concept of "cephalic shock" as a somatic link to Winnicott's "False Self" (2008; 2011); and Guy Tonella (2008; 2011) has done this using the resources of both Attachment Theory and Stern's developmental psychology of the Self in his ESMER model to incorporate these primitive energetic and sensory elements into a new paradigm for Bioenergetic therapy.

I have been exploring the Kleinian/Bionian/Grotstein/Ogden object relations line of development to try to find a theoretical base which dynamically explains the kinds of transference phenomena described above, and which can also incorporate Lowen's elaborations of the energetic and sensory levels of psychic and somatic functioning.

Object relations theory stands alongside ego psychology, interpersonal psychoanalysis, self psychology, and attachment theory as one of the key historical lines of psychoanalytic thought. Ogden (1996, p. 194) has pointed out how each line has its own epistemology and its own methodology. Each has arisen historically as their key theoreticians, e.g. Freud, Hartmann, Sullivan, Kohut, Bowlby, Klein etc., have considered different kinds of human experiences filtered through their own efforts to understand their patients (and themselves).

Object relations theory[4] can be traced back to Ferenczi's idea of "introjection"[5], but it was Fairbairn who first reformulated drive theory to show that libido was not pleasure-seeking but object-seeking[6] (Mitchell, 1995, p. 115). Fairbairn also replaced Freud's structural model[7] of the mind with a model of an unconscious inner world composed of a

4 For an in-depth theoretical study of object relations theory, read Ogden (2004, esp. Ch. 6).

5 Freud had first used the word "projection" and it was Ferenczi who first used the concept of "introjection" to describe how the "neurotic helps himself by *taking into the ego* ... a part of the world". (Brown, 2011, p. 22).

6 The word "object", first used by Freud, can be confusing. Its meaning is clearer if you substitute the word "person" in relation to "external objects". Grotstein (2009, p. 160) suggests the words "demon", "phantom", "presences", or "other subjects" in relation to "internal objects".

7 Lowen used Freud's structural model (id, ego, superego) in his explication of Bioenergetic Analysis. One could argue that object relations theory draws more on Freud's topographical model (unconscious, pre-conscious, conscious) than on the structural model. Read Brown (2011, p. 27f.) for how these different models affected approaches to countertransference in the history of Psychoanalysis.

central self (ego) with split-off and repressed parts of the self (ego sub-organizations), that enter into object relationships with each other, e.g. the "internal saboteur" attacking the "loving (libidinal) self" (Ogden, 2010, p. 101).

Melanie Klein[8], true to Freud's notions of the libidinal and death instincts, saw the drives, not as pleasure-seeking, but as a way of experiencing oneself as "good" or "bad". The instinct to love (libido) has embedded within it, a pre-conception of a loving object, just as the impulse to destroy (death instinct) has a pre-conception of an aggressive, hateful object. And so, the infant's first internal representations (objects), resulting from pleasant and unpleasant sensory and affective experiences that activate these pre-conceptions, are of a "good breast" that lovingly feeds him and makes him feel good, and of a "bad breast" that hatefully feeds him bad milk, giving him a belly-ache and making him feel persecuted. The repeated subjective experience of good and bad objects are continuously being *introjected* from and *projected* into the body of the mother. Not only the objects, but also the infant's ego ("I-ness"), have to be omnipotently split apart to protect the "good" from the persecutory "bad" through a process of unconscious phantasy[9]. This gives rise to the *paranoid-schizoid* position. As the infant develops the capacity to tolerate both his goodness and his badness (love and hate) he emerges from the *paranoid-schizoid* position into the *depressive* position. If the infant has "good enough" mothering he comes to realize his mother is not just a breast (a "part-object", not separate from himself, that he has magically, or omnipotently controlled), but also a person (a "whole-object", separate from himself), and in his *guilt* he tries to make *reparation* to her. This position is called *depressive* because the infant not only feels guilt, mourning, and the need to make reparation, but he experiences the *ambivalence* of whole-person relating, having to contain and deal with contradictory psyche/somatic impulses and perceptions in the real world, where things are not "all good" or "all bad".

The ways these phantasised split-objects and split-ego relate with each

---

8 It is not difficult to dismiss Klein's contribution because of some of her wilder speculations and her personality. Winnicott called her a "Eureka Shrieker", as she was always proclaiming something new. However, the works of Bion, Grotstein, the Barangers, Ferro, Ogden and others have shown the profound usefulness of many of her basic insights and formulations.

9 In psychoanalytic terms, "phantasy" is a production of the unconscious. It differs from "fantasy", which is a production of the imagination. Some authors use the word "fantasy" for both productions.

other ("object relations") are seen, in the Kleinian world, as the primary way people structure their minds. The infant's unconscious phantasised internal relationships between the split-objects and split-ego are primary and more powerful than even the parental environment, which is only of secondary importance. These "object relations" endure into adulthood acting as templates for experiences and relationships in the external world. The internal objects and the internal object relations are what are projected in transference situations.

Klein's views were challenged by Fairbairn, Winnicott, Guntrip, the British Independents, and by Bowlby. These writers gave much more importance to the actual, not phantasised, parent/child relationship, discounted the death instinct[10], and provided theoretically coherent concepts of internal object relations involving subdivisions of the self (e.g. Fairbairn's "ego sub-organizations" and Winnicott's "True Self and False Self").

While there is still a strong post-Kleinian tradition in London, which draws on the original object relations insights of Melanie Klein and is refining her basic ideas (Grotstein, 2009, p. xiii), a significant development occurred in 1968 when Wilfred Bion, a Kleinian, emigrated from London to Los Angeles. Bion developed Klein's ideas in a unique way that has given rise to exciting psychoanalytic developments in South America, Italy and California.

This paper draws heavily on the writings of James Grotstein and Thomas Ogden, both of whom live in California. Grotstein, who was in analysis with Bion in Los Angeles for six years, is perhaps today's clearest exponent of Bion's ideas. He has advanced many of Bion's ideas in a way that shows the complex dynamic relationship between the unconscious and the conscious mind, first discovered by Freud. Ogden[11], drawing on a range of views, has shown how Klein *"introduced a new perspective from which to organize clinical and metapsychological thinking"* (2004, p. 137). While Ogden integrates Klein's basic perspective into his own revisionary reading of Freud, he has also highlighted the theoretical fallacies in several of her formulations. More importantly, he has integrated the contributions of Bion, Fairbairn and Winnicott and created a modern object relations theory.

10 For a detailed critique of the Kleinian "death instinct" read Guntrip (1968, pp. 413–417) and Grotstein (2009, Vol 1, p. 194f. & p. 308).

11 Ogden has developed his own unique form of object relations theory, using a dialectical framework. A study of Ogden's writings is richly rewarding. It is worth noting that Reich (1929), as a Marxist, was the first person to systematically use dialectical thinking in psychoanalysis and this "antithetical" thinking is also present in Lowen's writings.

A close reading of Ogden also reveals the inclusion of his own somatic awareness in his clinical practice.

Wilfred Bion is of great interest to me because he developed some of Melanie Klein's views in ways that I believe resonate with Reich's "primary energetic functioning" (Davis, 2008, p. 15) and with Lowen's insights into the *"great wells of feeling which lie at the core of human beings"*. Bion, as a psychoanalyst, unlike Reich and Lowen, is perhaps on the "mind"[12] side of the Cartesian mind/body split, although many of his metaphors have a strong energetic, somatic, sensory and motoric feel to them that make them accessible and relevant to bioenergetic theory and practice.

My belief is that Reich's notion of "orgone energy" and Lowen's compelling energetic and somatic perceptions into the depths of the human core may be analogous to Bion's insights into the raw, inherent, unknowable Absolute Truth (which he termed "O"), and to his concept of "beta (β) elements". These latter are raw, concrete, unprocessed sensory and emotional imprints of "O", that are "muscularly", or "forcefully" processed by expelling them (through projective identification) into another. Reich, Lowen and Bion all believed that the primary energy underpinning our human existence is unknowable and only becomes manifest at the level of sensation and emotion in the psyche/soma.

Like Lowen (1971, pp. 41–69), Bion was profoundly influenced by Freud's writings on the *pleasure principle* and the *reality principle* (Brown, 2011, p. 84). Freud had explained how the psychic apparatus unburdens itself from the "accretions of stimuli" (id forces) into the external world. The body (id forces) "makes demands" on the mind (Ogden, 2004, p. 18). The mind has to work, or "to think" (adapt to reality) to find expression for the "id" tensions that fill the body and demand gratification (pleasure). Bion elaborated these ideas of Freud to show how the raw, concrete somatic/sensory experiences (beta (β) elements) can be transformed into meaningful affective experiences allowing us to think, to dream, to feel, and to symbolize reality. Bion called this transformative process the "alpha (α) function", allowing us to verbally encode and symbolically process sensory impressions and also traumatic experiences.

Lowen follows Reich in describing the same processes that Freud and Bion are describing. For Reich, "the *first* impulse of *every* creature must be a

12 Bion, like Reich and Lowen, saw the patient in a unitary manner: "*I have talked about the body and mind as if they are two entirely different things. I don't believe it. ...the patient is one, a whole, a complete person.*" (2005, p. 38).

desire to establish contact with the outer world". This arises from the biopsychic unity of the person, and the discharge of energy (id force) is impossible without contact with the world (Reich, 1972, p. 271). Reich in his work with schizophrenics showed how emotions are bio-energetic, plasmatic functions that come before mental functions, before meaningfulness, speech and other higher functions of the organism, and Lowen took the same position (Reich, 1972, p. 445; Lowen, 1971, p. 363). Their position is fully in accord with Bion's, who also gained his insights from his work with psychotic patients, into how the higher functions of the mind, such as thinking, symbolizing and narrative develop from concrete sensory experiences (beta (β) elements)[13].

Bion also introduces an intersubjective dimension to this process of transforming sensory/emotional concrete experience into symbolically encoded thoughts (Brown, 2011, p. 119). Bion (1962), using the Kleinian framework of introjection and projection, understood the mother to be a container for the unprocessed sensory experiences (the contained) of the infant, and that the task of the mother is to experience the full effect (Mitrani, 2001, p. 165) of these projected dysregulated psyche-somatic energetic experiences of both ecstasy and rage/panic (Tustin, 1992, p. 170). The mother, or perhaps the "mothering" parent, is then able to transform these projections, which she has introjected from the baby, and gradually return them to the infant, decontaminated of their dysregulated intensities through her "alpha (α) function". And it is this basic human process that we can call normal "transference and countertransference" communication, or what Grotstein (2009, Vol.1, p. 225) has called "projective (trans-)identification[14] as a means of communication between infant/analysand and the mother/analyst".

Grotstein (2009, Vol.1, p. 225) has also identified many types of transference and countertransference, which he ultimately sees, and perhaps energetically describes, as "the exorcism of demons" – a description, which fits well with one of my vignettes. I would like to outline three of the key transferences.

13 This epigenetic development parallels Tonella's ESMER paradigm. Interestingly, Balestriere (2007), a French psychoanalyst working with psychotic patients, writes about the centrality of "sensoriality" in the formation of representations and pictograms.

14 The "(trans)" insertion between the words "projective" and "identification" signifies that the communication is external, between two people, rather than between the internal representations (objects) of the patient.

Neurotic Transference

I think we are all familiar with the general idea of transference, where a feeling state from the past is ambiguously projected into the therapeutic relationship, "distorting" the patient's view of the therapist (Ogden, 1991, p. 2). It is "ambiguous" because the patient is both relating to the therapist as a person, and yet the therapist is reminding them of some aspect of a past relationship that they are attempting to preserve in the therapeutic relationship (Ogden, 1990, p. 90). Neurotic transferences, arising from the oedipal stage of development, usually have characteristic feelings of anxiety, jealousy, rivalry and guilt arising from ambivalent triangular relationships (Ogden, 1990, p. 119). Lowen's elucidation of neurotic transferences within the various character structures remains a valuable resource for our deeper understanding of transference at the oedipal level.

Projective Identification As a Means of Communication

"Projective identification" is a stronger form of transference than neurotic transference. As well as "distortion", the patient exerts unconscious "pressure", or "coercion" (Ogden, 1991, p. 2; 1990, p. 151) on the therapist to experience himself as if he were one of the patient's internal or external objects. For instance, in the vignette of my going to sleep, I unconsciously experienced the pressure to become, and did become, the patient's father (one of his internal objects) and did not wake up to the deep reality in the therapy room. I was "possessed" or taken over by the patient's unconscious phantasy, and experienced *"the pressure to think, feel and behave in a manner congruent with the projection"* (Ogden, 1991, p. 12).

In projective identification, then, the unprocessed, or dysregulated sensory and affective elements that make up the patient's object world are unconsciously projected by the patient and unconsciously introjected by the therapist, both persons using energetic, somatic, sensory, and visceral non-verbal cues to communicate (Schore, 2003, p. 280). The therapist can then act like the "good enough parent" and partially metabolize or digest these elements, and return them to the patient in a form that can be digested and incorporated, rather like a sea-bird regurgitating semi-digested fish for its young.

As noted above, it was Bion who broadened Klein's (1946) original concept of "projective identification" from being an internal "schizoid mechanism" into being the most important mechanism by which a patient communicates his inner world to the therapist. For Bion, projective identification is not just an intrapersonal phantasy, it is an interpersonal interaction (Ogden, 1991, p. 26). It is also the process that describes the normal communication between an infant and mother, allowing the infant's sensory/emotional experiences (beta (β) elements) to be transformed by the mother's alpha (α) function (Grotstein, 2009, Vol.1, p. 273). Bion pointed out the pathological consequences if neither the infant nor the mother allows this process to occur, resulting in the destruction of the links that allow learning from experience to occur.

Ogden (1991, pp. 1–9) points out that projective identification is not a metapsychological concept; it is a clinical-level conceptualization that can be phenomenologically verified and observed, e.g. through the therapist's countertransferential experiences (as in my vignettes).

Projective Identification in the Paranoid-Schizoid Position

It was Melanie Klein who first made the distinction between the "paranoid-schizoid" and the "depressive" positions[15]. Klein, who was an incapable mother of infants herself (Grosskurth 1986, p. 49f.), and rather a depressive and domineering person, was also a genius at understanding the psychological dynamics of young children and interpreting their play using classical adult psychoanalytic interpretations. Many writers credit her with being the first to open up the psychic life of infants to an in-depth psychoanalytic understanding.

Paranoid-schizoid refers to the earliest mental activity of the infant before there is the capacity of the child to be aware of itself or its parent as a person, or before there is the capacity for psychological functioning. It is paranoid because one is endangered by the omnipotent and omniscient forces arising from a dysregulated or even malevolent environment (for Kleinians, it is the "death instinct", rather than the environment, that generates destructive

15 Ogden (1989, p. 30f.; 1996, p. 33f.) has proposed an earlier position, the "contiguous-autistic" position that gives rise to primitive experiences of having (or not) a sensory boundary or "sensory floor". Tustin's amazing work (1992) with autistic children reveals the experience of raw terror of a voided sensory boundary. The three positions give rise to different types of experience, each having its own type of anxiety, defences, object relatedness, forms of symbolization, quality of subjectivity and subjective experience of the body.

and persecutory infantile phantasies); it is schizoid because there is a splitting of the endangered from the endangering, or the distancing of goodness and badness, e.g. in the vignette about the Garden of Eden, the patient is eternally trapped in "goodness", having omnipotently split herself off from the possibility of knowing "badness", and thus from the possibility of becoming fully human; and it is called projective identification because one is able to project the split-off elements into another person and experience them safely at a distance (Ogden, 1990, p. 65), e.g. as in the vignette of my going to sleep. The depressive position refers to the emergence from that state into human time and space, and it is "depressive" as there is now awareness of the ambiguity of whole-person-to-person relationships and of the ability to both hurt and be hurt and to make reparation.

Ogden (1990, p. 118) has pointed out that Freud eloquently said, "*Wo Es war, soll Ich werden*" – "Where It was, there (an) I shall be". This succinctly makes the distinction between Melanie Klein's "paranoid-schizoid" and "depressive" positions. There is no "I-ness", only "It-ness", in the paranoid-schizoid position, and no real person-to-person relationships are possible.

I believe that bioenergetic therapists need to be aware of transferences, or projective identifications, arising from the paranoid-schizoid position, as these transferences can have very strong energetic and sensory/somatic resonances (Bion's beta (β) elements), and as we know, Lowen focused much of his theory and clinical practice on developing therapists' capacity to work with these energetic and somatic forces and feelings "which lie at the core of human beings".

Transference in the paranoid-schizoid position is based on the complete separation of love and hate, or good and bad, which generates experiences that are not of this ordinary world. It is like being in a fog on a strange planet and being paranoid and fearful of omnipotently destructive forces or entities, as in the vignette of evil entities and archangels. Alternatively, with split-off love, there can be ecstatic experiences of omnipotent love. I have written about having to hold onto my chair to stop myself being magnetically sucked into a spiritual and sexual merger with a patient (2008, p. 20).

With a paranoid-schizoid transference there can be a strange sort of energy (beta (β) elements) present that stops a person from being able to think; there is an air of being captured in a way that is not quite nameable and that cannot be fully described psychologically. By definition, there is no interpreting self available, and no meanings can be assigned to perceptions; they just are. Previously shared experiences count for nothing, and everything has "to start all over again". History is being rewritten all the time to keep the loving and hating aspects split off. Phenomenological time and history does not exist. Nothing happens in real time. For the patient and the therapist, there can be a sense of discontinuity or amnesia for what happened previously. As a therapist, you may feel numb, dumb and useless (Ogden, 2009, p. 98) and find it difficult to centre yourself in your own somatic reality. This may happen in the course of one session, or it may be a subtle pattern over time, having much less intense features than what I have described. The therapist has to both let herself experience the numb, unable to think, state of being, and also be able "shake (herself) out of this numbing feeling of reality" (Bion, quoted in Ogden, 2009, p. 98) and transform herself into a new way of being able to think for and with the patient. This primitive merger state is evident in several of my vignettes.

Mitrani (2001, p. 165) has pointed out how the therapist/mother does this for the patient. "*This assumes a mother/analyst who has her own boundaries, internal space, a capacity to bear pain, to contemplate, to think and reflect back.*" The effect on the patient is an increased "*capacity to make meaning, increased mental space, and the development of a mind that can think for itself*". We need to add, "and fully possess a body that they can live in".

It is important to view these powerful transference phenomena constructively as core wounding is at stake. These transference phenomena are the means by which the patient projects his/her split-off hatred or love into a therapist who can metabolize and help transform these dark or ecstatic forces (beta (β) elements) into something more "human", ordinary and bearable, just as the "good enough mother" does for her baby (the alpha (α) function).

I think it is essential in somatic therapy that we are aware of the distinctions between these levels of transference. To work at this depth not only requires good supervision, where the supervisor can support the therapist to "bear these states", it sometimes also requires the therapist to undertake therapy to loosen the grip of their own schizoid and oral issues triggered by immersion in these powerful force fields.

Case Presentation

I would like to present a case of my work with a young man who was stuck in a paranoid-schizoid world. He also had areas of health that helped him form a strong therapeutic positive transference with me, and together we worked to successfully help him emerge into a more ordinary and satisfying existence, or into the "depressive position"[16].

I worked with Russell[17], aged 32, for four years. He was a young businessman. Classically he presented as a narcissistic personality with very strong intellectual defences. His parents separated when he was 14 years. He abhorred his father and three siblings for deserting his mother. He felt very protective of his mother, but persecuted by her, as she was extremely paranoid, believing that he was sending emails to strangers each day telling them her business. She bombarded him with emails about his father's family, repeating the same old historical complaints week after week, year in, year out. He repeatedly told her that he would not respond to this type of email, but to no avail, nothing ever changed.

When I first met him, his forehead, which he described as "his atomic bomb shelter", was large, prominent and hot, and his eyes were like tiny lights at the back of a cave. His face looked like a baby's face. When he got stressed, he was aware of a force like a steel helmet descending over his forehead from the back of his head. His chest was very broad and as flat as a board, but sometimes completely concave from shoulder to shoulder. His upper back was quite hunched with pooled rage. He had a slim waist and strong legs. He had a black belt in martial arts. He described his torso as layered: in front is a layer of asphalt road, then a layer of grief, then a void, and his back is made of steel with large metal rods protruding outwards and inwards. When he accessed strong feelings, his whole body quaked, and bubbles of air jerkily spasmed out of him. He then became bent over double with the pain of a locked diaphragm and needed to be in the corner by himself, impervious to any help from me. His physical and psychic agony was sometimes hardly bearable for himself or for me.

He was not able to maintain a relationship with a woman for more than a few months, and after a short while, he would suffer sexual im-

16 It is beyond the scope of this paper to expand on the dialectical relationship between the paranoid-schizoid and the depressive positions, and the temporal/atemporal (diachronic/synchronic) relationship between them. Read Ogden (1996, pp. 33–39). In short, the "subject" is to be found in the dialectically tensive space between them. This dialectical process is operative between the conscious and unconscious systems, just as it is in Reich and Lowen's "antithetical" relationship between psyche and soma.

17 "Russell" is a pseudonym. The patient has given permission for this material to be published.

potency. When he hugged people, he would hold them away with his arms, and be nearly side-on to the person he was making contact with. His ideal relationship with a woman was one where he could predict what would be happening precisely for the next 30 years, but it was also on the condition that if he found his true love, he would have to present her to his mother, and if she disapproved, he would have to give up his dream partner.

Therapy was difficult as he had the image of his life-force being like a tiny ember under a pile of cold ashes. Any attempt to blow on the ember with bodywork was met with strong somatic and intellectual resistance. He had a dream of being alone in a violent Saharan sandstorm, with no way forward, only the possibility of crawling back to an old landmark hill that contained a cave in which his mother sat. There was no possibility of his being found.

In my early work with him, I did not understand the concept of the paranoid-schizoid position. I tape-recorded a therapy session in the first year of work with him in which he clearly identified his experiences in this state of being, and it is fascinating listening to this session now with the benefit of a theoretical understanding of the paranoid-schizoid position.

On the tape-recording of the session he discusses:

- how every day has to begin anew – "starting all over again". Yesterday has gone. There is no sense of continuity of experience – history is static and has to begin again;
- his fear and paranoia, and the parallels between his and his mother's life – neither of them are able to sustain a relationship, and both have "to start all over again";
- yet somehow he knows "we are going to make it" (as in the song, "Starting All Over Again"). He has enough health and has a trusting connection with me, so he is sure we are going to make it;
- he has "inherited" (he had no choice) his mother's pattern of anger, paranoia, and pushing people away;
- in the session he actually moves into the paranoid-schizoid state and he becomes very distressed. He is aware all his life situations have become "merged". He feels he has to "buy into" his mother's state of being. One can feel the lost little boy in an "It-world", in his struggling words and in his efforts to find his breath against the suffocating internal somatic and psychic pressure;
- he is aware his mother is lost, sinking away, going down into an "It-world" where she is not available for relationship, and he joins her,

with the strange logic, "that if two are lost, they are less lost, and I'll be with her"[18];

- he then gets a memory flash of when he was 11 years old, and his mother was actually going "down" to the railway station. He has an intense feeling she is endangered, he's freaking out, and he goes "down" to join her. He finds her safe, but there is no relationship available in which he can say, person to person, "I was worried about you". She is in her own "It-world", one that he can resonate with, but he cannot communicate with her;
- but at least he is aware that he is available for relationship, and that they are "walking back up" from the "It-world", back from the danger of the railway station to home.

Progress was made, after about three more years of somatic and analytic work. He was finally able to let go control and "kick the shit" out of cushions and pummel them as if they were his mother, and perhaps succeeding, for the very first time, in forging a somatopsychic boundary between himself and his mother. He then had a session where he was aware of an immense "psychic column of grief" just out in front of him, and that he had been carrying this burden of grief that existed in his mother's family for nearly 100 years[19]. This burden concerned a baby girl who was pivotal in the family history of migration from England to New Zealand. The baby had been abandoned in order for the family "to start all over again" in a new country. I felt fully absorbed in this extended dramatic history, as though I were in a movie.

For the first three years or so, despite the strong positive transference and countertransference, there seemed to be a strong resistance on his part, and on mine, to being aware of any negative transference and countertransference in the room (Mitrani, 2001, p. 6). However, following the sessions where he expressed his rage and grief in relation to his mother, I was able to work more directly with the negative transference. I became aware he was very angry with me, and encouraged him to express his feelings about me.

18 A good example of "altruistic identification" a form of forceful projective identification (Bion) associated with Faimberg's "telescoping of generations" (Brown, 2011, p. 227).

19 For an example of the "telescoping of generations" (Faimberg) read footnote 18. I am indebted to Odila Weigand (personal communication, February 2011) for drawing attention to Hellinger's "Systemic Constellations" for an alternative view of this phenomenon.

There were several sessions where his body would nearly leap out of his chair in unconscious impulses to attack me. Finally he was able to close his eyes and tell me that he was going to kill me, and it would happen so fast I wouldn't even know he'd done it. As he was a martial arts expert, physically he could have done this. He was able to visualize doing it, his muscles rippling with energy and his body jerking, with spasms of breath coming from the depths of his belly. I was both able to hang onto present reality so that I was physically safe, and also to be present with him in a timeless sort of space in which there was danger in the electrified air. When he opened his eyes, he beheld a miracle – I was still there, he hadn't destroyed me. He just couldn't believe it. He was absolutely amazed. We were both alive and there was a sense of deep connection and ordinariness between us.

That session was pivotal, and he often referred back to that moment in the following months. He had emerged from an "It-world" nightmare into an "I-world". He had emerged from the "paranoid-schizoid" position into the "depressive" position. He was able to be in relationship. The difference between the two states was palpable, and it started being evident in his work and social relationships over the next several months. His visage changed into a more mature look, with his forehead not so prominent, eyes more out in his face, and he soon met a lovely woman who seemed like a partner "made in heaven" for him. They are still happily together.

For myself as therapist, I also felt released from the pressure of strong countertransferential unconscious energies, e. g. release from the dread that perhaps "we were not going to make it" after several years of hopelessly "starting all over again"; release from my split-off negativity towards him arising from the failure of my best bioenergetic interventions; release from my impotent rage in his refusal to work with his rage at his "bad" father; and release from my secret narcissism at his enduring positive projection onto me as a "good" father. Overall, I felt released from the unconscious countertransferential pressure to keep "goodness" and "badness" completely split apart, and then the great relief to once again feel "ordinary".

Discussion

A key question for me has been whether one can introduce a different line of psychoanalytic thought, other than ego psychology, into Bioenergetic Analysis without compromising the latter's integrity. Does introducing object relations theory damage the inheritance we have received from Alexander Lowen?

I have been helped to resolve this by re-reading the Preface and 1st Chapter of *Language of the Body.* There, Lowen (1971, p. xii) has outlined the three key elements that distinguishes bioenergetics from psychoanalysis, namely:

1. the unitary study of the patient's psychological problem as manifested in body structure and movement;
2. the systematic release of chronic muscular tension;
3. the relationship between therapist and patient involves verbal and physical techniques, which add a depth, not found in psychoanalysis, bringing transferential and countertransferential issues more sharply into focus.

There is nothing in these three essential elements that ties them exclusively to drive theory and oedipal dynamics, i.e. ego psychology. I believe that each of them can be understood from an object relations perspective without diminishing the nature or effectiveness of Bioenergetic Analysis.

In fact, there are signs of Lowen's three key elements (minus the physical techniques, of course) in the work of Ogden, who allows the patient's deep somatic/sensory reality "to possess" his own somatic reality, even to the point where he reports experiencing himself as dreadfully ill or dying. He does this as part of his "reverie" experience in helping the patient transform somatic/sensory states into embodied symbolic experiences. Ogden's (2001, p. 155) elegant statement that *"the experience of being bodied and the experience of being minded are inseparable qualities of the unitary experience of being alive"*, captures his appreciation of the need to "re-mind the body" and "embody the mind". He knows that sensations stemming from the body can not only overwhelm a person's sanity but their very being. Mental activity, split off from the body, becomes "hypertrophied"[20], omnipotently controlling *"everything that happens in the experience of the body, as well as in relationships to external and internal objects"* (2001, p. 156). This resonates with our common experience of ourselves and our patients – the split between mind and body. It is what makes bioenergetics such a central therapeutic modality in the restoration of *"the unitary*

20 HYPERTROPHY N. Enlargement (*of* organ etc.) due to excessive nutrition. (Concise Oxford Dictionary. This term was first used by Bion (1962).

experience of being alive" and the discovery that "*you are your body*". This is a key area where Bioenergetic Analysis can make a real contribution to modern psychoanalysis. This is also illustrated in the case study.

The three essential elements of bioenergetics necessarily require, as Hilton (1988, p. 60) first pointed out, an embodied intersubjective dimension (involving transferential and countertransferential phenomena) when working with the pre-oedipal issues of schizoid, oral and borderline personality organisations. These chronic somatic contractions and the resultant psychological defences were formed within a dysregulated, and even toxic or malevolent parent/child relationship, and can only be effectively healed within a "Relational Somatic Psychotherapy" (Hilton, 2008), where the intersubjective relationship can bear the kind of states I have alluded to in discussing Bion's "beta (β) elements". Again, the case study shows the metabolizing of early overwhelming affective states at the core of object relations theory can also be effective in understanding and guiding the systematic release of chronic muscular tensions using verbal and physical techniques to restore the psyche/somatic unity of the person.

We know that Lowen's view on the "faulted" nature of countertransference reflected his belief that working directly with the body demands a "greater ability" (1971, p. xiii) on the part of a bioenergetic therapist than it does of a psychoanalyst. But does that really mean that ALL countertransference is "faulted", i. e. that it is only the therapist's unresolved issues, and that there is no place for it in the healing process? Lowen's rejection of countertransference came, not only from his insights into the power of Bioenergetic Analysis, but from his elaboration of ego psychology, which he had inherited from Reich. Ego psychology was the dominant psychoanalytic framework in the USA from the 1940's until the 1970's (Makari, 2008, p. 482), so it is probably not surprising that Lowen, as a therapist in the 1950/60's, needing to communicate the power, depth and relevance of Bioenergetic Analysis, chose ego psychology as the most appropriate intellectual framework for this task.

Is Bioenergetic Analysis irrevocably tied to ego psychology? Many of our writers in Europe, the United States and South America, such as Clauer (2007), Finlay (1999), Hilton (2008), Klopstech (2008; 2009), Koemeda-Lutz (2011), Lewis (2007; 2008; 2011), Resneck-Sannes (2005), Schroeter (2009), Tonella (2008; 2011), Tuccillo (2006), Weigand (2001), Zaccagnini (2011), and many others, have already answered that by the incorporation of other intellectual frameworks into Bioenergetic Analysis.

In this article I have attempted to do something similar by the use of object relations theory in critiquing those elements of Lowen's bioenergetics that I believe are no longer theoretically able to fully explain pre-oedipal transference and countertransference phenomena. I have tried to recover the essence of Lowen's insights into the energetic/sensory power of "analysis from below", by showing how Bion's ideas of "beta (β) elements" and "container/contained" can bring an intersubjective dimension to in-depth bioenergetic therapy; and I have shown in the case study how Lowen's three definitional elements can be operationalized by the use of object relations theory within Bioenergetic Analysis.

Conclusion

The French psychoanalyst, André Green has said, *"I can see no advantage to be gained from constructing a psychoanalytic theory totally freed from knowledge of the soma"* (2005, p. 276). And I am suggesting that our knowledge of soma cannot be totally freed from the knowledge of the object representations of the mind. Our approach is called Bioenergetic Analysis. We will not lose our connection with the body and with Lowen's rich inheritance through learning from current psychoanalytic reflections in our pursuit of *"the truth of the body"*. And, at the same time, we can make a valuable contribution to psychoanalytic thought by demonstrating the embodiment of the mind in Bioenergetic Analysis.

This paper has shown how one particular theoretical line of object relations theory can be used to more fully inform Bioenergetic Analysis as to the nature of pre-oedipal transference and countertransference, for the benefit of our patients.

Dedication

I would like to dedicate this article to my supervisor, Diane Zwimpfer MA(APP), Dip Psychotherapy, MNZAP(APC), MANZAP, to whom I am indebted for my understanding of the paranoid-schizoid and depressive positions, and whose unconditional support has enabled me to work bioenergetically and psychodynamically with powerful transference and countertransference phenomena.

References

Balestriere, L. (2007): The work of the psychoanalyst in the field of psychosis. International Journal of Psycho-Analysis 88, 407–421.

Bion, W. (1962): Learning from Experience. Heinemann, London.

Bion, W. (1977): Seven Servants: Four Works. Jason Aronson, New York.

Bion, W. (2005): The Italian Seminars. Karnac, London.

Brown, L. (2011): Intersubjective Processes and the Unconscious: An Integration of Freudian, Kleinian and Bionian Perspectives. Routledge, New York.

Clauer, J. (2007): Embodied Comprehension: Treatment of Psychosomatic Disorders in Bioenergetic Analysis. The Clinical Journal for Bioenergetic Analysis 17, 105–133.

Cockburn, G. (2008a): Standing on Both Legs. The Clinical Journal for Bioenergetic Analysis 18, 11–26.

Cockburn, G. (2008b): Survival and Transformation in the Oral/Oedipal Vortex. The European Journal of Bioenergetic Analysis and Psychotherapy 4, 1, 6–31.

Davis, W. (2008): On Working Energetically, Part 1. www.functionalanalysis.de. (Accessed 8 April 2011).

Finlay, D. (1999): A Relational Approach to Bioenergetics. The Clinical Journal for Bioenergetic Analysis 10, 2, 35–52.

Freud, S. (1910): The future prospects of psycho-analytic therapy. Standard Edition 11. The Hogarth Press, London.

Freud, S. (1912): Papers on Technique. Standard Edition 12. The Hogarth Press, London.

Green, A. (2005): Key Ideas for a Contemporary Psychoanalysis. Routledge, London.

Grosskurth, P. (1986): Melanie Klein, Her World and Her Work. Knopf, New York.

Grotstein, J. (2007): A Beam of Intense Darkness: Wilfred Bion's Legacy to Psychoanalysis. Karnac, London.

Grotstein, J. (2009): ... But At the Same Time and On Another Level. 2 Vols. Karnac, London.

Guntrip, H. (1968): Schizoid Phenomena, Object-Relations and the Self. Hogarth Press, London.

Heimann, P (1950): On counter-transference. International Journal of Psycho-Analysis 31:81–84.

Hilton, R. (1988): Narcissism and the Therapist's Resistance. The Clinical Journal for Bioenergetic Analysis 3, 2, 45–75.

Hilton, R. (2008): Relational Somatic Psychotherapy: Collected Essays of Robert Hilton, Ph.D. Sieck, M. (ed). Santa Barbara Graduate Institute.

Klein, M. (1946): Notes on Some Schizoid Mechanisms. In: Envy and Gratitude and Other Works 1946–1963. (1975). Free Press, New York.

Klein, M. (1975): The Psycho-Analysis of Children. Free Press, New York.

Klein, M. (1975): Love, Guilt and Reparation and Other Works 1921–1945. Free Press, New York.

Klopstech, A. (2008): Bioenergetic Analysis and Contemporary Psychotherapy: Further Considerations. The Clinical Journal for Bioenergetic Analysis 18, 114–136.

Klopstech, A. (2009): So Which Body Is It? The Clinical Journal for Bioenergetic Analysis 19, 11–30.

Koemeda-Lutz, M. (2011): The Relative Contribution of Cognition, Affect and Motor Behavior in Psychotherapeutic Processes: Empathy and Interaction as Healing Factors. In: Heinrich-Clauer, V. (ed): Handbook Bioenergetic Analysis. Psychosozial-Verlag, Gießen. 469–490.

Lewis, R. (2007): Bioenergetics in Search of a Secure Self. The Clinical Journal for Bioenergetic Analysis 17, 135–164.

Lewis, R. (2008): The clinical theory of Lowen, his mentor Reich, and possibly all of us in the field, as seen from a personal perspective. The USA Body Psychotherapy Journal 7, 1, 35–59.

Lewis, R. (2011): Cephalic Shock as a Somatic Link to the False Self Personality. In: Heinrich-Clauer, V. (ed): Handbook Bioenergetic Analysis. Psychosozial-Verlag, Gießen. 113–128.

Lowen, A. (1969): The Betrayal of the Body. Macmillan Publishing Co., New York.

Lowen, A. (1971): The Language of the Body. Macmillan Publishing Co., New York.

Lowen, A. (1975): Bioenergetics. Penguin Books, New York.

Lowen, A. (1995): The Process of Bioenergetics. The Clinical Journal for Bioenergetic Analysis 6, 1, 1–8.

Lowen, A. (1996): Keynote Address. The Clinical Journal for Bioenergetic Analysis 7, 1, 1–15.

Lowen, A. (2004): Honoring the Body. Bioenergetics Press, Alachua.

Makari, G. (2008): Revolution in Mind. Harper Collins Publishers, New York.

Mitchell, S., & Black, M. (1995): Freud and Beyond: A History of Psychoanalytic Thought. Basic Books, New York.

Mitrani, J. (2001): Ordinary People and Extra-Ordinary Protections. Routledge, New York.

Ogden, T. (1989): The Primitive Edge of Experience. Jason Aronson, New York.

Ogden, T. (1990): The Matrix of the Mind. Jason Aronson, New York.

Ogden, T. (1991): Projective Identification & Psychotherapeutic Technique. Jason Aronson, New York.

Ogden, T. (1994): The analytic third-working with intersubjective clinical facts. International Journal of Psycho-Analysis 75, 3–20.

Ogden, T. (1996): The Subjects of Analysis. Jason Aronson, New York.

Ogden, T. (2001): Reminding the Body. In: Conversations at the Frontier of Dreaming. Jason Aronson, New York.

Ogden, T. (2004): The Matrix of the Mind. Jason Aronson, New York.

Ogden, T. (2009): Rediscovering Psychoanalysis. Routledge, New York.

Ogden, T. (2010): Why Read Fairbairn? International Journal of Psycho-Analysis 91, 101–118.

Reich, A. (1951): On counter-transference. International Journal of Psycho-Analysis 32, 25–31.

Reich, W. (1929): Dialectical Materialism and Psychoanalysis. In: Baxandall, L. (1972). (ed): Sex-Pol Essays, 1929–34. Vintage Books, New York.

Reich, W. (1991): Character Analysis. The Noonday Press, New York.

Resneck-Sannes, H. (2005): Bioenergetics: Past, Present and Future. The Clinical Journal for Bioenergetic Analysis 15, 33–54.

Schore, A. (2003): Affect Regulation and the Repair of the Self. W. W. Norton & Co., New York.

Schroeter, V. (2009): Borderline Character Structure Revisited. The Clinical Journal for Bioenergetic Analysis 19, 31–52.

Slakter, E. (1987): Countertransference. Jason Aronson, New York.

Tonella, G. (2008): Paradigms for Bioenergetic Analysis at the Dawn of the 21st Century. The Clinical Journal for Bioenergetic Analysis 18, 27–60.

Tonella, G. (2011): The Self: Its Functions, its Attachments and its Interactions. In: Heinrich-Clauer, V. (ed): Handbook Bioenergetic Analysis. Psychosozial-Verlag, Gießen. 57–112.

Tuccillo, E. (2006): A Somatopsychic Relational Model for Growing an Emotionally Healthy, Sexually Open Body from the Ground Up. The Clinical Journal for Bioenergetic Analysis 16. 63–86.

Tustin, F. (1992): Autistic States in Children. Routledge, New York.
Weigand, O. (2001): Current Trends on Bioenergetic Therapy, Brazil. The Clinical Journal for Bioenergetic Analysis 12, 1, 87–100.
Zaccagnini, G. (2011): Affective Relationships and Bodily Process. In: Heinrich-Clauer, V. (ed): Handbook Bioenergetic Analysis. Psychosozial-Verlag, Gießen. 149–158.

About the Author

Garry Cockburn BSW(Hons), CBT, MNZAP(APC), was born in New Zealand, trained as a Catholic priest in Sydney, Australia in the 1960s, and undertook post-graduate studies in theology in Rome. After leaving the priesthood, he qualified as a social worker and worked in the New Zealand Government child abuse agency for nearly 30 years. He finished his bioenergetic training in 1995 and has worked in private practice as a bioenergetic therapist since 2002. He has published in the Bioenergetic Journal, and in the European J. for Bioenergetics and Psychotherapy. He was a keynote speaker at the Seville IIBA conference. He is a Local Trainer for the New Zealand Society and joined the Board of Trustees of the IIBA in 2011. E-mail: garry.cockburn@paradise.net.nz.

Integrating Brain, Mind, and Body: Clinical and Therapeutic Implications of Neuroscience

An Introduction[1]

Margit Koemeda-Lutz

Abstracts

English

This paper presents a tentative assessment of what Bioenergetic Therapists may take out of the proliferating neuroscientific findings of the past two to three decades. A few examples are picked to demonstrate that different levels of observation – the sociobehavioral, the psychodynamic, the physiological and the cellular-biochemical – are equally relevant to an understanding of the complexity of human experiencing, information processing and functioning. Interventions on any of these levels can induce change on the same and/or any of the other levels: an increase of subjectively experienced stress, an activation of certain promotors and genes, synthesis and release of certain hormones, aggressive behaviour etc. All these processes are interconnected in highly complex systems. A short case vignette at the end recommends that clinicians acquire as much scientifically based explicit knowledge as possible, but that in moment-to-moment interactions with their patients they must also rely on their intuition and what has become "implicit" in their personality as psychosomatically oriented therapists.

Key words: bioenergetic analysis, body psychotherapy, neuroscience, psychosomatics, complex systems

---

1 Keynote presented at the 21st biennial IIBA International Conference, October 26–30, 2011, San Diego, California.

Zur Integration von Gehirn, Geist und Körper: Klinische und Therapeutische Implikationen Neurowissenschaftlicher Forschungsergebnisse – Eine Einführung (German)

Dieser Beitrag versucht eine Bestandsaufname bezüglich des Nutzens der in den letzten zwei bis drei Jahrzehnten exponentiell angewachsenen neurowissenschaftlichen Forschungsergebnisse für Bioenergetische AnalytikerInnen. Einige ausgewählte Beispiele sollen verdeutlichen, dass verschiedene Ebenen der Beobachtung – die soziobehaviorale, die psychodynamische, die physiologische, die zellulär-biochemische – gleichermaßen relevant für ein Verständnis der Komplexität menschlicher Erfahrung, Informationsverarbeitung und menschlichen Funktionierens sind. Interventionen auf jeder dieser Ebenen können Veränderungen auf derselben und/ oder auf jeder anderen Ebene auslösen: ein erhöhtes subjektives Stresserleben, die Aktivierung bestimmter Promotoren und der entsprechenden Gene, die Synthese und Ausschüttung bestimmter Hormone, aggressives Verhalten usw. All diese Vorgänge sind in hoch komplexen Systemen miteinander verknüpft. Eine kurze Fallvignette am Ende empfiehlt, dass sich klinisch Arbeitende möglichst viel wissenschaftlich fundiertes explizites Wissen aneignen, sich aber in den von Moment-zu-Moment sich entfaltenden Interaktionen mit ihren PatientInnen auch auf ihre Intuition und das, was in ihrer Persönlichkeit als psychosomatisch Arbeitende "implizit" geworden ist, verlassen müssen.

Schlüsselwörter: Bioenergetische Analyse, Körperpsychotherapie, Neurowissenschaft, Psychosomatik, komplexe Systeme

Integrer cerveau, esprit et corps: Implications cliniques et thérapeutique des neuroscience – une introduction[2] (French)

Cet article présente une tentative d'évaluation de ce que les thérapeutes bioénergéticiens peuvent tirer de la prolifération des conclusions neuroscientifiques des deux ou trois décades passées. Quelques exemples sont choisis pour démontrer que différents niveaux d'évaluation – la socio

2 Présentation principale présentée à la 21ème Conférence Internationale biennale IIBA, 26–30 Octobre 2011, San Diego, Californie, USA.

behavioriste, la psycho-dynamique, la physiologique et biochimique cellulaire – sont également utiles pour une compréhension de la complexité de l'expérience humaine, le traitement et le fonctionnement de l'information. Les interventions à n'importe lequel de ces niveaux peuvent induire du changement au même et/ou à n'importe lequel des autres niveaux: une augmentation du stress expérimenté au niveau subjectif, une activation de certains organisateurs et gènes, synthèse et libération de certaines hormones, comportement agressif etc ... Tous ces processus sont interconnectés dans des systèmes extrêmement complexes. A la fin une courte vignette d'un cas recommande aux cliniciens d'acquérir une connaissance scientifique aussi explicite que possible, mais que dans leurs interactions dans l'instant avec leurs patients ils puissent aussi faire confiance à leur intuition et avec ce qui est devenu "implicite" dans leur personnalité en tant que thérapeutes orientés vers la psychosomatique.

Mots Clés: Analyse Bioenergétique, psychothérapie corporelle, neuroscience, psychosomatique, systèmes complexes

Integrando el cerebro, la mente y el cuerpo: Implicaciones clínicas y terapéuticas de la neurociencia – Una introducción (Spanish)

Este artículo presenta un intento de evaluación de lo que los analistas bioenergéticos pueden obtener de los crecientes hallazgos neurocientíficos de las dos o tres últimas décadas. Se muestran algunos ejemplos para demostrar que distintos niveles de observación – el socioconductista, el psicodinámico, el fisiológico y el bioquímico-celular – son igualmente relevantes para una comprensión de la complejidad de la experiencia humana y el procesamiento y funcionamiento de la información. Intervenciones en cualquiera de estos niveles pueden inducir cambios en el mismo y/o en cualquiera de los otros niveles: un aumento de stress experimentado subjetivamente, una activación de ciertos promotores y genes, síntesis y liberación de ciertas hormonas, comportamiento agresivo, etc. Todos estos procesos están interconectados en sistemas altamente complejos. La viñeta de un caso al final recomienda que los clínicos adquieran tanto conocimiento científico explícito como sea posible, pero que en las interacciones momento-a-momento con sus pacientes también deben confiar en su intuición y en lo que se ha convertido en "implícito" en su personalidad como terapeutas con orientación psicosomática.

Conceptos clave: neurociencia, celular-bioquímico, hormonas, explícito, implícito

Integrare il cervello, la mente e il corpo: conseguenze cliniche e terapeutiche delle neuroscienze – un'introduzione (Italian)[3]

Questo scritto presenta il tentativo di valutare cosa un terapeuta bioenergetico può trarre dalle ricerche neuroscientifiche degli ultimi venti o trent'anni. Vengono portati alcuni esempi per dimostrare che diversi livelli di osservazione – quella sociocomportamentale, la psicodinamica, quella fisiologica e biochimica-cellulare – sono ugualmente rilevanti per la comprensione della complessità dell'esperienza umana, del funzionamento e del modo di processare le informazioni. Interventi su ognuno di questi livelli possono indurre cambiamenti sullo stesso e/o su qualcuno degli altri livelli: l'incremento dello stress soggettivamente sperimentato, l'attivazione di alcuni geni e promotori, la sintesi ed il rilascio di alcuni ormoni, il comportamento aggressivo ecc. Tutti questi processi sono interconnessi in sistemi altamente complessi. Una breve vignetta clinica raccomanda che i clinici acquisiscano quanta più possibile conoscenza esplicita scientificamente basata, ma che nelle loro interazioni con i pazienti debbono anche far assegnamento sul loro intuito e su ciò che è diventato implicito in quanto terapeuti psico-corporei.

Parole chiave: neuroscienze, biochimico-cellulare, ormoni dello stress, esplicito, implicito

3 Relazione presentata al 21° Congresso biennale dell'IIBA, 26–30 Ottobre 2011, San Diego, California.

Integrando Cérebro, Mente e Corpo: Implicações clinicas e terapeuticas da Neurociência – una Introdução (Portuguese)[4]

Este artigo apresenta uma contribuição experimental do que terapeutas bioenergéticos podem extrair da multiplicidade de descobertas neurocientíficas das duas ou três últimas décadas.

Alguns exemplos foram selecionados para demonstrar que diferentes níveis de observação – sócio-comportamental, psicodinâmico, fisiológico e bioquímico-celular – são igualmente relevantes para a compreensão da complexidade da experiência humana e do processamento e funcionamento da informação.

Intervenções em qualquer desses níveis podem induzir mudanças nos mesmos e/ou em outros níveis como: aumento do stress subjetivamente experienciado, ativação de certos promotores e genes, síntese e liberação de certos hormônios, comportamento agressivo, etc. Todos esses processos estão interligados em sistemas altamente complexos.

Um pequeno estudo de caso no fim do artigo recomenda que os clínicos aprofundem ao máximo seu conhecimento do explícito baseado cientificamente, mas que em interações momento-a-momento com seus clientes, confiem em sua intuição e no que se tornou "implícito" em sua personalidade como terapeutas psicossomaticamente orientados.

Palavras-chave: Neurociência, celular-bioquímico, estresse, explicito, implícito

The past two to three decades have been witnessing a worldwide boom in the neurosciences. National and other funds have generously invested in this development. Psychiatric and psychotherapeutic clinicians have eagerly received new findings in this field, and neurobiologically informed models of human functioning and change have become "standard".

The 21st biennial International IIBA Conference, recently held at San Diego, was therefore dedicated to an exploration of the clinical and therapeutic implications of recent neuroscientific findings for Bioenergetic Therapists, who work with embodied human beings.

4 Palestra apresentada no 21° Congresso Internacional bienal do IIBA – Outubro, 26–30, 2011, San Diego.

Originally, Joachim Bauer, professor for psychoneuroimmunology at the University of Freiburg in Germany, had agreed to present two keynotes, one on "Genes as Biological Communicators – the Impact of Relational Experience on the Activity of our Genes", based on his book of 2002, the other one on "Mirror Neurons as a Neurobiological Basis for Intuition", based on a book of 2005. Bauer's professional training and expertise cover Internal Medicine, Psychiatry, Neurobiology and Psychosomatic Medicine. He initiated and carried out significant research in the fields of gene regulation and immunology, on Alzheimer's disease and Depression. In his books he accomplishes the difficult task of relating the details of microbiological knowledge to the more general questions of clinical psychiatry and psychotherapy.

Unfortunately, four weeks before the conference, Joachim Bauer had to cancel his flight for sudden serious health problems, as he told us.

In the seventies of the last century there were fierce debates about the relative importance of nature versus nurture. In a Time Life Books issue on "The Genetic Code" from 1994, the preface still contends that the genetic blueprint determines the somatic appearance of individuals as well as their intelligence and temperament.

From current neurobiological findings, especially the field of epigenetics, we learn that heredity explains only a very small proportion of interindividual variation. Human beings share the same genetic blueprints to the incredible amount of 99.9%! The obvious variation between individuals therefore must be due to the **interaction** between environmental, including cellular and proprioceptive signals and genes.

According to current knowledge, only 1–2% of all human diseases are caused by gene mutations. The overwhelming "remainder" is due to dysfunctional communication processes on biological, social and/or psychological systemic levels. Also, it is certain substances or environmental factors, as e.g. nutrition, perceived relational situations, ultraviolet radiation, and transcription factors etc., that absorb or activate promoters, i.e. regulatory sequences on specific genes.

The Human Genome Project was accomplished in 2000. It had decoded the totality of all human genes – comprising over 3 billion nucleotides. Genetic "texts", i.e. DNS sequences, are fixed for each organism and subject to hereditary processes. The "expression" and activity of most genes though is subject to regulation in interaction with "contextual" and environmental stimuli and is a continuing, life long process. Individual experiences provoke and form reaction patterns that influence this regulation.

One level of observation, where epigenetics is relevant, is neuronal information processing. Our brain "translates" sensory into biological input. Nerve cells get stimulated and genes in these cells become activated. They elicit the production and release of neurotransmitters, growth factors or hormones and cause nerve cells to grow or decline. Active synapses enhance their structure, while inactive synapses dissolve ("Use it or loose it"). Frequent and intense experiences strengthen the interconnection of cell assemblies. Simultaneous, synchronic, rhythmical bioelectric activities (ca. 40 Hz) in cells create networks ("Cells that fire together, wire together").

Neuroscientific findings taught us that perceptions and notions are based on synaptic connections between nerve cells and that mental operations are facilitated by the interconnections of nerve cell assemblies. In addition, we learned that the neuronal architecture of our brains is subject to change throughout our lives. The good news to us psychotherapists is that it is therefore never too late for psychotherapeutic work! Here may be a connection to the rapidly growing field of gerontopsychotherapy.

In his book, Bauer reviews and reflects on an immense body of microbiological, psychiatric and psychosomatic research literature to demonstrate how life experiences, especially early in life, interact with the genetically designed human potential, in order to shape individual personalities on different levels – mental, emotional, behavioural, physiological and morphological levels.

He further demonstrates that – more than anything – interpersonal relationships influence somatic processes. This influence reaches as "deep" as to the regulation of gene activity. It is effective in adult human beings, and even more so during infancy and prenatal development.

As psychotherapists we KNOW that early experiences shape our feeling, thinking and behavioural patterns. But neurobiological research has demonstrated that early experiences also shape our somatic functioning, such as physiological patterns and the neuronal architecture in our brains. Attuned positive bonding in early childhood protects stress genes from over-reactivity in later life. Positive human relationships constitute the best "medication without side effects" (Bauer 2002, p. 13) for coping with psychic and somatic stress.

Early in life neuronal networks develop that later determine how a person appraises his or her environment and how he or she copes with challenging events. The architecture of neuronal networks and their functional patterns depend on early (relational) experiences. If they are positive, they foster resilience, if they are detrimental (like e.g. neglect, abuse, violence), they may lead to dissociative patterns and contribute as etiological factors to the evolution of psychiatric disorders.

Integrating brain, mind and body means to perceive our clients and interact with them on several different levels, most of them beyond our consciousness. There are biochemical, cellular, behavioural and psychological changes in each of the participating organisms involved. None of these levels is more essential than any of the others. Processes on each of these levels influence each other, bottom-up and top-down and evolve parallel in time.

The question whether psychiatry and psychotherapy should be a natural or a philosophical science has been debated since Sigmund Freud's time and one may doubt if it will ever be settled. While in the sixties and seventies of the past century the social sciences boomed and prospered, the nineties of the last and the first decade of the 21st century shifted to more emphasis on the natural sciences. Most likely, we need both perspectives. And psychosomatic orientations in psychotherapy – Bioenergetic Analysis is one of its prominent exponents – are especially predisposed to integrate both aspects.

The following paragraphs will, on the basis of four short examples, delineate what we may have learned from the neurosciences lately.

Neurobiological Aspects of Stress Reactions

In a series of animal studies, Canadian stress researchers working with Michael Meaney found that maternal attention and love, operationalized as the amount of time spent with licking, cuddling, touching etc., significantly influenced their offspring's biological stress system. In intensely mothered animal babies, stress-gene (CRH) activation was lower later in life under standardized stress conditions than in animals that had been poorly mothered as newborns; and growth (BNDF-producing) gene activation, which is a prerequisite for successful learning, was higher.

Such findings are relevant to us bioenergetic therapists if we assume that we may make inferences from animal studies to human beings and that similar mechanisms are at work in us. Secondly, we must claim that psychotherapy provides for similar resources as does parental bonding and love and therefore may influence our patients' epigenetic functioning in a way that they become less vulnerable to stress and increase their resilience in coping with life. We KNEW that intuitively before, didn't we? But neuroscientific findings have provided empirical proof that when we experience stress, in our brain (more precisely: in the hypothalamus) genes get activated that produce corticotropine-releasing hormones (CRH). This activation then triggers a whole cascade of further reactions. A second kind of genes (POMC) in our pituary gland is then activated, producing proopiomelanocortine, which in turn produces adrenocorticotropic hormones (ACTH). These are then released into our blood circulation. They then spread throughout our body and initiate the production and release of cortisol in our adrenal glands. Current cortisol levels in turn modulate CRH production in the hypothalamus. All this (and more) happens within a few minutes after having been exposed to stressful stimulation. Actually, it is even more complicated than this – my description only refers to the left part of figure 1.

Psychoneuroimmunological Aspects of Stress-Induced Inflammatory Reactions

In addition to endocrine reactions, stress also impacts the immune system. The immune system consists of two subtypes – an innate one (comprising granulocytes, macrophages, dendritic cells and natural killer cells) and an acquired one (comprising B-(bone marrow) and T-Lymphocytes), the latter being characterized by adaptive learning and shaping by stochastic genetic recombination in the thyroid gland in order to effectively meet and bind intruding antigenic material.

Psychological stress activates the sympathetic division of the autonomic nervous system and at the same time triggers (among many other things) inflammatory activities in the immune system. As pointed out earlier, it also activates the HPA-stress-axis, which triggers an antagonistic reaction in the immune system in order to confine the inflammatory reaction (TH1/TH2 shift), protecting the organism from an overreaction. These interacting processes can derail at several points. Either the endocrine part (HPA-axis) is not sensitive enough to immunological activation or immune cells are not sensitive to the inhibitory effects of glucocorticoids, e.g. cortisol. The inflammatory reaction can not be limited with detrimental

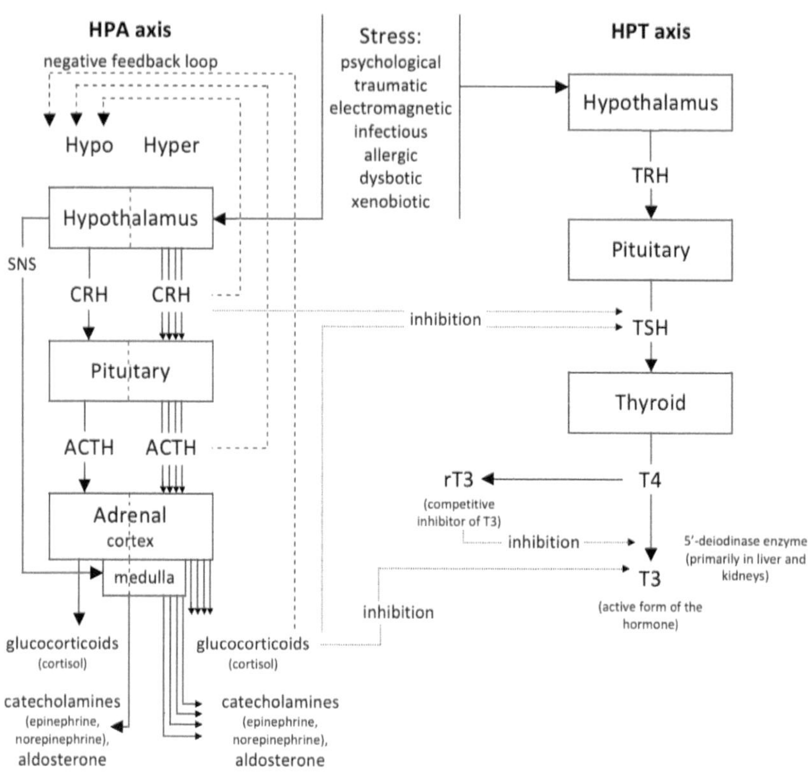

Figure 1: HPA and HPT Axes
HPA Axis = Hypothalamic Pituitary Adrenal Axis
HPT Axis = Hypothalamic Pituitary Thyroid Axis
CRH = Corticotrophic Releasing Hormone
ACTH = Adrenocorticotrophic Hormone
TRH = Thyroid Releasing Hormone
TSH = Thyroid Stimulating Hormone
rT3 = Reverse T3

long term effects on the organism (Besedovsky and del Rey 2007, cit. after Schubert 2011, p. 76). Schubert speculates that premature exhaustion of the stress system and a consecutive development of inflammatory diseases (like polyarthritis, multiple sclerosis etc.) may be due to imprints early in life, even prenatally. In San Diego there is a long-term study on Adverse

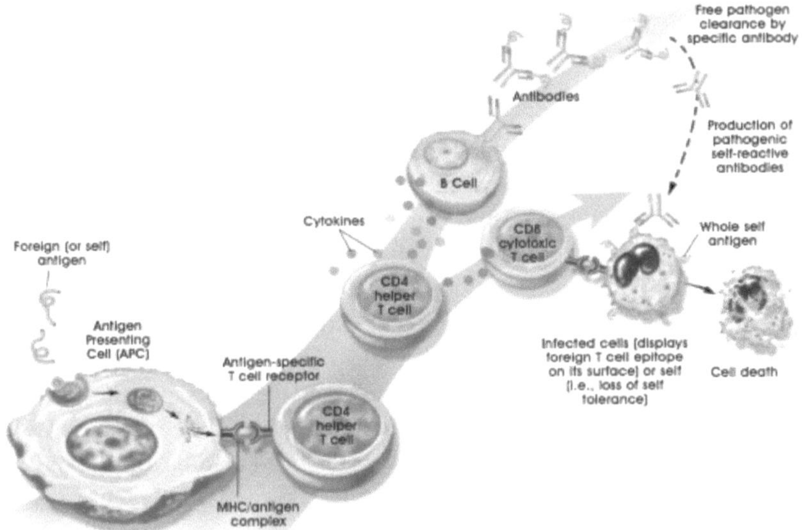

Figure 2

Childhood Experience (ACE) carried out by the Southern California Permanent Medical Group (Felitti et al. 1998, cit. after Schubert 2011) who try to follow up the effects of adverse childhood experiences to health and illness in adult life.

This was a second example of how a subjectively experienced process is connected to physiological processes. Next, a third example of the interrelatedness of processes at different levels of observation is provided.

Hypocapnia States

Bioenergetic Therapists work with exercises designed to induce stress and arousal in the autonomic nervous system. In a pilot study (Müller & Koemeda-Lutz 2004) at the State Hospital Münsterlingen we could demonstrate that, for instance, the "Backwards Bow" (figure 3), as well as induced hyperventilation, elicited a state of hypocapnia. As an indicator we took Carbon Dioxide concentrations in the blood, as measured transcutaneously.

Figure 3: Backwards Bow

Hypocapnia is defined as an increase in breathing volume (voluntary ventilation, deepened breathing), which causes an enlargement of the area of contact between the air and the pulmonary surface (number of capillaries) and through this increases the rate of exhalation of carbon-dioxide (CO_2). An increase in breath volume and rate increases the rate of gas exchange. The more air saturated with CO_2 is exhaled, the faster the external air can absorb additional CO_2. In this way the CO_2-concentration in the blood decreases.

During the "Backwards Bow" the mean CO_2-concentration dropped significantly (from 5.7 to 5.1 kPa (Kilo-Pascal)), and even more so with hyperventilation (down to 3.7 kPa). With muscle activity or expressive vocalizations, the CO_2-concentration rose back to normal. During the "elephant"(also known as "forward bend"; figure 4) exercise the breathing deepened and vibrations in the leg muscles became visible, but a hypocapnia state did not emerge.

Figure 4: Elephant/Forward Bend

From a neurological point of view, hypocapnia causes states of ANS-excitability and reduces modulating and inhibiting influences from the cortex. Limbically dominated modes of processing prevail, which can, for instance, lead to emotional arousal.

Clinical Bioenergetic-Analytic experience has repeatedly demonstrated that the previously mentioned exercises lead to a loosening of affective defenses and make way for chronically suppressed emotions to be expressed. By interacting with the therapist, corrective experiences can be made – for instance, the client might say, "The therapist does not get angry when I express my rage, she does not abandon me", or the like. Such experiences create new entries in the emotional experiential memory and are paralleled by physiological changes that can be traced.

Emotions – Psychosomatic Phenomena

Working with emotions is essential to bioenergetic therapy. Most psychopathological disorders imply emotional dysfunction. According to Thoits (1985, cit. in Berking 2008) 85% of all disorders listed in DSM-IV (Saß et al. 2000) have at least one emotion-related criterion as one of their constituents. Emotions are truly psychosomatic phenomena. Subjective feelings on one side parallel somatic processes on the other side, i.e. the Autonomic Nervous System (figure 5), the somatic nervous and muscular system (figure 6), the Endocrine System (figure 7), and the Immune Organs (figure 8).

The chances are good that if we help a patient to heal her emotional life, this will be paralleled by positive changes on all the other levels of her embodied being. To summarize, most perceptions are processed unconsciously and our nervous system initiates or triggers many psychic and somatic reactions without our awareness.

Stress in so-called civilized societies is mainly caused by interpersonal conflicts and lack of social support, as when needs and desires are not communicated, or by offenses, hurt and humiliation. As clinicians we may be familiar with the Hypothalamus-pituitary and adrenal gland-stress axis and its regulatory functions in cortisol synthesis and release. But that this stress system is individually coined in every single organism may not have been so widely known. In addition to raised cortisol levels, stress also causes the release of other transmitters noxious to nerve cells, e.g. adrenaline, noradrenalin and glutamate. Increased cortisol and glutamate concentrations in the brain can cause cell decline, especially in the hippocampus, which is responsible for memory functions.

Cortisol has lasting effects on the immune system, blocks interleukins and tumor necrosis factor. Under prolonged stress, these immunological transmitters are no longer produced in sufficient quantities because cortisol blocks important genes responsible for their production.

Stress increases the susceptibility for virus infections. Cortisol represses fever and other important defence reactions necessary for healing. Stress can have negative effects on the course of several diseases like multiple

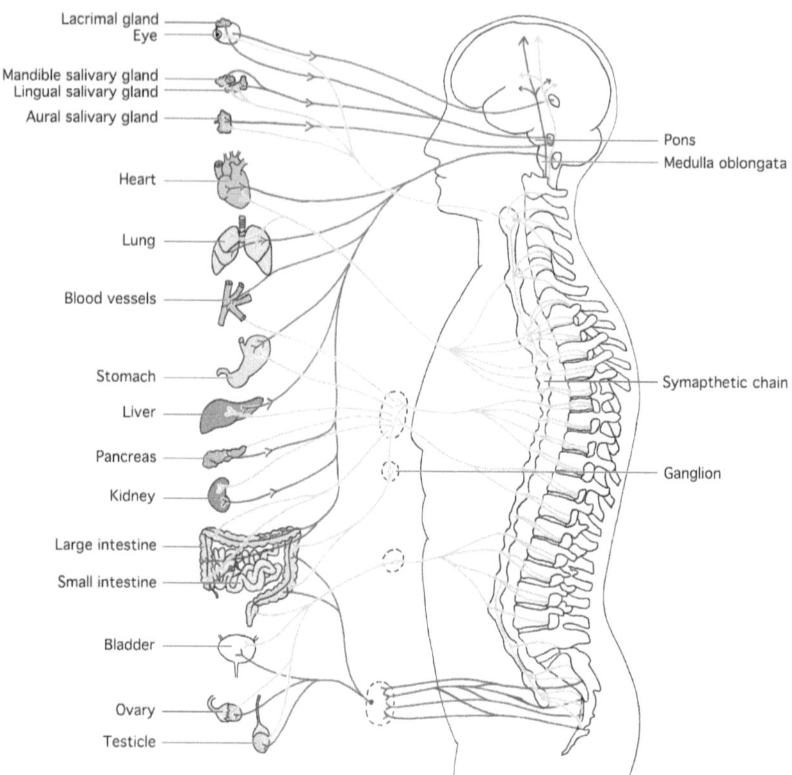

Figure 5: The Autonomic – Sympathetic and Parasympathetic – Nervous System

sclerosis, rheumatoid arthritis, skin diseases (like psoriasis), diabetes, and coronary and heart conditions.

Bauer and others have collected empirical evidence to demonstrate that positive relationships are biologically rooted health factors. When interpersonal relationships decrease quantitatively and qualitatively, health disorders increase.

In (body) psychotherapy we have different levels of intervention: On a biomedical level we can prescribe medication aiming, for instance, at an increase of intercellular serotonin. In this way – and it works on the biochemical and cellular level – we hope to enhance the patient's subjective feeling of well-being. On a psychological level we can help a patient to better become aware of and express his anger and by this means hope

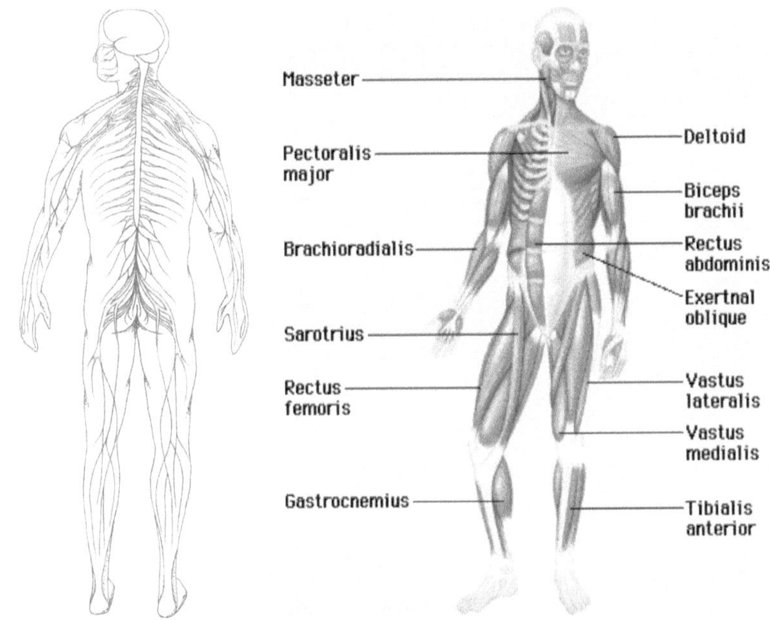

Figure 6: Somatic Nervous and Muscular System

to increase his interpersonal competence and at the same time possibly lower his blood pressure. On a behavioural level we can encourage a patient to quit her job which may result in burnout prevention, and at the same time enhance immune function. While interventions can be aimed at one systemic level, effects might be observed on the same and/or at other levels.

How does this apply to the most prevalent illnesses in Western societies: depression, coronary and heart disease, cancer, pain syndromes, post traumatic stress disorder and burnout states? Here is a brief outline, following Bauer's propositions:

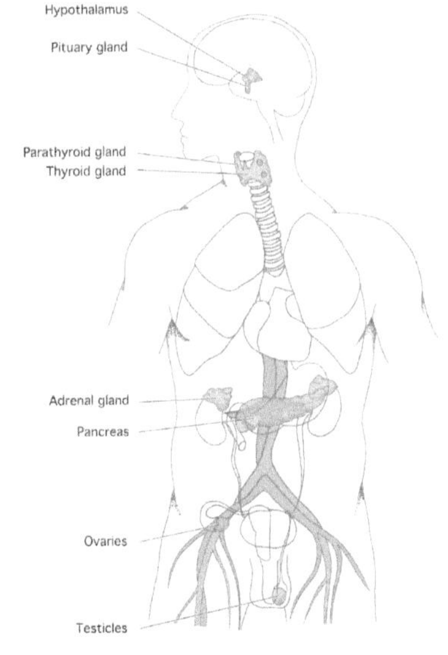

Figure 7: Immune System

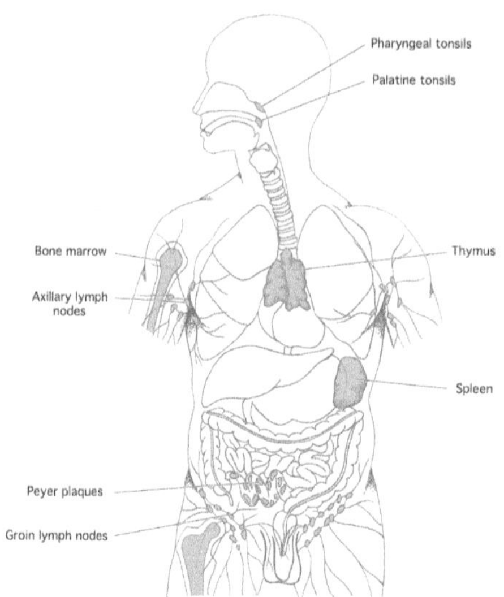

Figure 8: Endocrine System

Depression: Life events not only influence the well-being of a person, but substantially dysregulate gene activity and other somatic processes, resulting e.g. in sleep disorders, lack of motivation and agitation. With repeated depressive episodes there need not be any triggering events for a new episode any more. Depression is biologically conditioned. Depression is an over activation of the stress system. It has been demonstrated that depressive patients have significantly more problems and losses in their early relationships as compared to non-depressive controls.

Coronary and Heart Diseases: Several studies have shown the relationship between stress and depression and their influence on coronary and heart diseases. A combination of heart condition and depression bears a triple risk of mortality. Depression decreases heart rate variability and thereby increases the risk of heart disease.

Cancer: Stress and depression also influence the immunological defence and risk of tumor growth. Increased cortisol levels block immunological and inflammatory responses (reduction of natural killer cells). There exist studies which demonstrate that psychotherapeutic support reduces the risk of mortality.

Pain syndromes: Pain experiences leave imprints in our neuronal system like any other experiences. Pain leaves imprints specifically in the sensory area of the cortex and in the gyrus cinguli and facilitates future sensations of pain. Psychological and somatic pains "use" the same brain structures. Therefore psychological support and relaxation decrease the probability of pain sensations.

Post traumatic stress disorder (PTSD): In traumatic situations dissociation serves as a protective mechanism as genes for the production of endorphins are activated. The alarm reaction is stored in the amygdala and the person develops a chronic amygdaloid over-activity and exhibits an increased sensitization towards stress. This is often the starting point for dissociative disorders, borderline personality or eating disorders to evolve.

According to Bauer, several studies have demonstrated that psychotherapy is a method of healing which influences psyche and body at the same time. These results were from studies of verbal therapies under examination!

An important question for further inquiry will be: What benefit do we as clinicians have from increasing knowledge about the subconsciously functioning physiological and biochemical processes in human organisms? Are they the ultimate goal of our search for knowledge whereas concepts and theories on "higher" levels (as e.g. in psychology) are deficient and preliminary? Analyses on different levels have turned out to be worthwhile and these results may help us to shape and revise our concepts.

I would like to close with a case vignette.

Case vignette

A couple of weeks ago Laura came in for her 18th session, very frustrated, quite depressed and said: "I know I will fail, nothing works any more, my brain is on strike." She is a student at Zürich University, has accomplished writing and handing in her master's thesis, has passed a 3-day and another 4-hour written exam as well as an oral exam of 3 hours.

Her present task was to e-mail two additional theses with a short summary for their defence within the next two days to her professor, who was to see her for another oral exam the following week. Meanwhile I heard that she has passed all exams with excellent grades!

In that session I felt she had some anger underneath her depressed surface. How did I know? My mirror neurons must have told me: her overall muscle tone, some tiny movements around her mouth, the look of her eyes ... When I addressed this, she shrugged her shoulders, shook her head and said: "I don't want to go through all this a second time. If I fail this next exam, I will have to start all over again."

Up to this point our therapy had predominantly been some sort of coaching during the preparation for her exams. We had been discussing her theses. I asked questions which helped her clarify her own thoughts and arguments. While talking about topics of her field of expertise she usually regained self confidence and got reassured that she had acquired solid knowledge, which she was able to present and defend. On the basis of my empathic response connected to her frustrated and aggressive feelings, I suggested she express some of this. In this session I refrained from trying to help her formulate those two theses she needed and instead clenched my fists, raised them above my head, turned to the sofa next to my chair, hit on the pillow and said: "I feel pissed off. Ah!" then I added, "I really want to get out of this. I am fed up with this lonely studying business!"

She watched kind of disbelievingly. Then she nodded.

My post-hoc explanation: I had done this, hoping to trigger some neurons in her premotor cortex, serving as a model, so she could reconnect to her own self determination and her will to pass the last two exams.

Did I know at that point that she did NOT have a history of being subject to violent or abusive behaviour of others? I only guessed – because, if she had, my behaviour could have immediately thrown her back into a frozen state of immobilization and would have aggravated her present problems, even re-traumatized her.

My intuition then told me that she would have to do something with her head. She had mentioned that she really wanted to "switch" or even "tear off" her head. Expressive behaviour with her voice and her arms had not really connected her to her vital energy.

So I held up a cushion against the wall and suggested she kneel down in front of it and push with her head in order to "get through the wall". Triggered by this suggestion we found out that Laura was a caesarean baby. The rest of that session was spent simulating her birth process, whereby my hands served as the maternal cervix, gradually dilating while her vertex pushed against it. Later my whole body served as the maternal birth canal, which she was forcefully working herself through (I owe this kind of work to the pioneering work of William Emerson (e.g. 2011) and Karlton Terry (e.g. 2011)).

Totally to my surprise, at the end of this session, Laura pulled out of her purse seven typewritten pages, from which she read one paragraph to me. To my ears this was a perfect thesis for her next exam as her voice was firm, self confident and clear.

Was it helpful to me, the therapist, to know about mirror neurons, premotor and motor cortices, limbic systems, and the thalamus as a connecting center for incoming sensory data? All this neurobiological knowledge which I have acquired over the past 10–15 years, and which Bauer presents in his books with great expertise, is fascinating. It may have contributed to my decisions for the interventions in the described session above. But, during the process the leading part was probably not my cerebral cortex drawing from the storages of my explicit knowledge. I was certainly not directed by any theoretical knowledge of neurobiological functioning, but rather subconsciously driven by intuition and implicit knowledge, i.e. my own embodied experience as a human being and a bioenergetic clinician.

Conclusion

A fundamental principle of our universe is self similarity. We find analogies on all different levels of structure and functioning. Therefore, for effective psychotherapeutic work it is worthwhile studying different levels of organization in human beings. Symptoms and effects may be observed on any of these:

- If we help a patient to increase her assertiveness, we may also strengthen her immune system.
- If we are deeply empathic with another person who has to grieve a severe loss and teach her to limit grieving when needed, this is likely to change the dynamics of her cerebral blood flow.
- Relaxation training has been shown to correlate with increased cellular immunity (McGrady et al. 1992, cit. in Hall & Olnes 2011).
- But the connections are far more intricate and complex than simple causal relationships, as for example, I teach a person to express her anger and her lymphocyte titre goes up. However, the change in lymphocyte titre can be caused by an infection instead.

Since recent results from the neurosciences also inform us that most of our behaviour is not due to conscious decisions or our "free will" (e.g. Roth 1994, 2001, 2004; see also the startling Libet experiment, Kornhuber & Deecke 1965), we – bioenergetic clinicians – might as well continue to accumulate neuroscientific knowledge and clinical expertise, but then trust the subconsciously stored body of implicit knowledge to interact with our patients in the best way possible in each moment.

References

Bauer J (2002): Das Gedächtnis des Körpers – Wie Beziehungen und Lebensstile unsere Gene steuern. Frankfurt/M.: Eichborn.

Bauer J (2005): Warum ich fühle, was du fühlst – Intuitive Kommunikation und das Geheimnis der Spiegelneurone. Hamburg: Hoffmann und Campe.

Berking M (2008): Training emotionaler Kompetenzen. TEK – Schritt für Schritt. Heidelberg: Springer.

Besedovsky HO & del Rey A (2007): Physiology of Psychoneuroimmunology: A Personal View. Brain Behav Immun 21: 34–44; cit. in Schubert C (2011): Psychoneuroimmunologie körperlicher Erkrankungen, 66–109.

Emerson W (2011): Somatotrope Therapie. pp. 81–121 in Schindler P (Ed) Am Anfang des Lebens – Neue körperpsychotherapeutische Erkenntnisse über unsere frühesten Prägungen durch Schwangerschaft und Geburt. Basel: Schwabe.

Felitti VJ, Anda RF, Nordenberg D, Williamson DF, Spitz AM, Edwards V, Koss MP, Marks JS (1998): Relationship of Childhood Abuse and Household Dysfunction to Many of the Leading Causes of Death in Adults. The Adverse Childhood Experiences (ACE) Study. Am J Prev Med 14: 245–258; cit. in Schubert C (2011): Psychoneuroimmunologie körperlicher Erkrankungen, 66–109.

Hall HR & Olness K (2011): Hypnose, Imagination, Selbstregulierung und Immunaktiviät. 228–247 in Schubert C (2011) Psychoneuroimmunologie und Psychotherapie. Stuttgart: Schattauer.

Müller F & Koemeda-Lutz (2004): Pilotversuch zur Hypokapnie – Induktion durch bioenergetische Übungen am Kantonsspital Münsterlingen, Abt. Neurologie, unveröffentlicht.

Kornhuber HH & Deecke L (1965): Hirnpotentialänderungen bei Willkürbewegungen und passiven Bewegungen des Menschen: Bereitschaftspotential und reafferente Potentiale. Pflügers Archiv für Gesamte Physiologie 284: 1–17.

Mc Grady A, Conran P, Dickey D, Garman D, Farris E, Schumann-Brzezinski C (1992): The Effects of Biofeedback-Assisted Relaxation on Cell-Mediated Immunity, Cortisol, and White Blood Cell Count in Healthy Adult Subjects. J Behav Med 15: 343–54; cit. in Hall HR & Olness K (2011): Hypnose, Imagination, Selbstregulierung und Immunaktiviät. 228–247 in Schubert C (2011, Ed)

Roth G (1994): Das Gehirn und seine Wirklichkeit: kognitive Neurobiologie und ihre philosophischen Konsequenzen. Frankfurt/M.: Suhrkamp.

Roth G (2001): Fühlen, Denken, Handeln: Wie das Gehirn unser Verhalten steuert. Frankfurt/M.: Suhrkamp.

Roth G (2004): Das Verhältnis von bewusster und unbewusster Verhaltenssteuerung. Psychotherapie Forum. Themenheft: Neurowissenschaften und Psychotherapie. Koemeda-Lutz M (Hrsg) Wien: Springer Vol. 12 (2) 59–70.

Saß H, Wittchen HU & Zaudig M (2000): Diagnostisches und Statistisches Manual Psychischer Störungen DSM-IV (deutsche Bearbeitung). Göttingen: Hogrefe.

Schubert C (2011): Psychoneuroimmunologie und Psychotherapie. Stuttgart: Schattauer.

Terry K (2011): Die fünf Phasen der Spermienreise – einige psychologische Themen und Auswirkungen. pp. 143–167 in Schindler P (Ed) Am Anfang des Lebens – Neue körperpsychotherapeutische Erkenntnisse über unsere frühesten Prägungen durch Schwangerschaft und Geburt. Basel: Schwabe.

Thoits PA (1985): Self-labelling processes in mental illness: The role of emotional deviance. American Journal of Sociology 91 (2) 221–249.

About the Author

Margit Koemeda-Lutz, Dr. Dipl.Psych., is a licensed psychotherapist in private practice at Zürich and Ermatingen, Switzerland; she is coordinating trainer for the Swiss Society for Bioenergetic Analysis and Therapy (SGBAT) and faculty member of the International Institute for Bioenergetic Analysis (IIBA). She has been presenting and training in Switzerland, Austria, Germany and the USA. She has been a study group member in a neuropsychological research project at the University of Konstanz, FRG (1978–1985); founding member and co-organizer of annual psychotherapy conferences "Breitensteiner Psychotherapiewochen" (1981–2000); and member of the executive committee SGBAT (1994–2001). She is presently a member of the scientific committee of the Swiss Charter for Psychotherapy and author and editor of several books and articles on psychosomatic psychotherapy and its effectiveness (see www.sgbat.ch, www.bioenergetic-therapy.com and www.koemeda.ch).

Poem

Linda Neal

Describing or defining a poem always involves the risk of saying too much or too little. I'll say that "Toward Water" is a free-verse, unrhymed, lyric poem in five stanzas. To paraphrase W. H. Auden, if you're writing poems because you have a message for the world, forget it. If you're writing them because you love words, the sound of language and adventure, you're on the right track. So, I write a poem like I go on a trip. Language is the vehicle. The process is the destination. Though a poem (like "Toward Water,") has a kind of organic unity of images, a storyline or theme, the end comes as a surprise to me, and likewise probably to the reader as well. That's how a poem works – kind of like a good bioenergetic session.

Toward Water

On this cold November morning
I sit at the window, with my hot coffee
looking out at the nearby pine,
its branches spread out against the sky
its cones hanging on by the hundreds.
One thuds to the damp morning ground.
A squirrel cracks another in her jaw
but our destinies do not intertwine
even though when I was eight I shinnied
up bark in old jeans. The season didn't matter.

Because truth came down
to my childhood classroom
a Mason jar standing on an oak table
in the corner
and inside an embryo
floating
delivered into water
dead
like the contraction
in the pit of my stomach
when my mother walked in.

I expanded in rain
sloshing through puddles
alongside bones and coins
wearing red rubber boots
knowing
trees and water
as hedges against
my parents' dark weather
the muddy confluence of family strife.

At night in the dark
came the merging of the one with the many
the small with the large.
Some nights I became so small
I could hide inside a drop of water
and becoming water
be the whole ocean,
be everywhere at once
see my grandmother's grandmother
washing her black hair in a lake
and myself, safe and small
inside my mother,
before I entered the plains
of daughterhood and danger.

Safe in salty water,
alone and becoming
I could thrum a string
for the one who was to learn
no safety, not even, especially not
in the net of family.
Fished out of that warm and private sea
thrown up on dry land
I have looked for water
wherever I go, and exposed
to darker energies of close kin
I trek down
to damp sand, swim in the sea
search for wet valleys
sit at the mouths of caves
and the edges of waterfalls
exploring the flooded wilderness
of my life
absorbing the pulse of water,
learning
life not as a maze but a labyrinth.

About the Author

Linda Neal, MFT lives and works in Redondo Beach California. Her writing has appeared in a number of journals and newspapers, and she is currently working on a novel and memoir. She completed the bioenergetic training in 2003. She can be reached via email at lindarneal@gmail.com and by telephone at 310-540-2291.

Book Review

Bend Into Shape: Techniques for Bioenergetic Therapists

Jacqueline Mills

Bend Into Shape: Techniques for Bioenergetic Therapists[1], by Vincentia Schroeter, PhD and Barbara Thomson, PhD, is a treasure trove for bioenergetic therapists, whether they are certified or in an IIBA approved training program. This book looks at the multilayered approach bioenergetic analysis takes to helping people heal from a variety of presenting issues and breaks it down into digestible parts no matter where your starting place.

What I love about this book is that it is to the point. The authors make sure to say what they mean simply and directly and get to the heart of the treatment issues that all bioenergetic therapists encounter. Even better, they offer a plethora of techniques with illumination as to when, why and how to use them. They have also taken the time to articulate things we need to be cautious about and things we need to watch for, which I am sure comes out of their combined vast experience both in working with clients and in training therapists seeking bioenergetic certification. These "caution" and "watch for" sections are set apart in boxes which

1 *Bend Into Shape: Techniques for Bioenergetic Therapists*, was published in October 2011. The second edition is available at vincentiaschroeterphd.com.

makes for easy identification and inclusion into the practitioner's awareness.

In the first chapter they clearly state the ethical concerns of a body-based approach to psychotherapy. In the second chapter, Doctors Schroeter and Thompson talk about energy from a bioenergetic perspective, reviewing the unique contributions of Wilhelm Reich, Alexander Lowen and Robert Hilton. The third chapter is a rich description of the purpose of assessment techniques and details about how to read the body in both the natural pose and the charged pose. This includes an explanation of the exaggerated body stance and how moving from the exaggerated contracted posture to the exaggerated reverse posture "often reveals a hidden, unconscious aspect of the self that is in conflict with the preferred adaptive or contracted style." What follows is an explanation of assessing aggression, reaching, and alignment before going into detailed descriptions, including illustrations, of the stress positions. The last area of assessment in chapter three is relational assessment where the authors offer several techniques. The next six chapters cover the character structures, which are schizoid, oral, borderline, narcissist, masochist, and rigid. For each of these character structure chapters, the authors have given us an illustration of that structure's posture, the Hilton diagram depicting both the mental and the body adaptation, a description of how the character develops, what the potential transference and countertransference issues might be, tension patterns with the breath and techniques for working with the breath, and each character structure's relationship with grounding, energy, relational issues, expression, and sexuality, and techniques for working bioenergetically with each of the aforementioned areas. The visual summary of techniques by character types showing and describing blocks and then "corrective" techniques is a great reference!

Chapter ten covers special issues including developmental and acute trauma, shame, abuse and anxiety, where the authors share bioenergetic techniques and helpful clinical examples. Chapter eleven is organized similarly with a focus on special populations including eating disorders, medical conditions and chronic pain, alcohol and drugs, children, seniors and couples. Chapter twelve is rich with techniques by body segment and techniques by emotional issues make up chapter thirteen. These last two chapters are great for quick reference on very specific interventions either by body segment or emotional issue.

In my opinion, the authors have more than achieved their goal of providing a source of techniques for Bioenergetic therapists and students. To say that they have been thorough is an understatement. While their disclaimer is true that they could not, of course, include every intervention available, I have found this book to be an extraordinary resource. Not only for it's content, which is incredibly helpful, but also for the way in which it is organized. It is a great reference guide and educational tool chock full of intelligent information!

About the Author

Jacqueline Mills, PsyD, is a licensed marriage and family therapist with a private practice in Hermosa Beach, California. She received her doctorate in psychoanalysis from the Institute of Contemporary Psychoanalysis and trained at the Southern California Institute for Bioenergetic Analysis, becoming a Certified Bioenergetic Therapist (CBT) in January 2011.

The Expression of an Age-Old Need for Company

Infant Research and Bioenergetic Analysis

Nicoletta Cinotti

Abstracts

English

This article aims to explore the subject of the dialogue between bioenergetic analysis and infant research. The *still-face* paradigm will be introduced, allowing the processes of self-regulation and interactive regulation to be explored, as well as the bodily root of emotion regulation, and showing a way to use the results of scientific research to enrich our clinical and training resources. Theoretical exposition will be followed by the presentation of a short clinical study, which illustrates the possibility of intervention using this paradigm.

Key words: self-regulation, still-face, interactive regulation, dyadic state of consciousness

Säuglingsforschung und Bioenergetische Analyse: Ausdruck eines uralten Bedürfnisses nach Gemeinsamkeit (German)

Dieser Artikel hat das Ziel, die Verbindungen zwischen Bioenergetischer Analyse und Säuglingsforschung herauszuarbeiten. Dazu wird das Still-Face-Experiment vorgestellt. Mit ihm können die Wechselwirkungen zwischen Selbstregulation und Interaktiver Regulierung sowie gleichzeitig auch die körperlichen Grundlagen der Emotionsregulation untersucht werden.

Die Autorin zeigt anhand des Still-Face-Paradigmas, wie die Ergebnisse dieser wissenschaftlichen Untersuchungen ihre klinische Arbeitsweise und die Unterrichtsmöglichkeiten innerhalb der Bioenergetischen Analyse bereichert haben. Die theoretische Darstellung wird dann durch einen kurzen klinischen Fall ergänzt. Er veranschaulicht die Interventionsmöglichkeiten, welche die Anwendung der Still-Face-Paradigmas bietet.

Schlüsselwörter: Selbstregulation, Still-Face, Interaktive Regulation, Dyadische Bewusstseinszustände

Le tres ancien besoin de compagnie: Recherche l'enfant et l'analyse bioenergetique (French)

Cet article a pour but d'explorer le sujet du dialogue entre l'analyse bioénergétique et la recherche sur le jeune enfant. Le paradigme "still face" sera amené, ce qui permettra l'exploration des processus d'auto-régulation et de régulation interactive ainsi que celle de la racine corporelle de la régulation de l'émotion, il montrera une façon d'utiliser les résultats de la recherche scientifique pour enrichir nos ressource clinique et d'enseignement. La présentation théorique sera suivie par celle d'un bref cas clinique qui illustre la possibilité d'une intervention utilisant ce paradigme.

Mots clés: auto-régulation, still face, régulation interactive, état de conscience dyadique

La expresión de una antigua necesidad de acompañamiento: La investigación infantil y el análisis bioenergético (Spanish)

Este artículo explora el tema del diálogo entre el análisis bioenergético y la investigación infantil. Se introducirá el paradigma de la cara inmóvil, permitiendo explorar los procesos de auto-regulación y de regulación interactiva, así como la raíz corporal de la regulación emocional, y mostrando un modo para utilizar los resultados de la investigación científica a fin de enriquecer nuestros recursos clínicos y de formación. A la exposición teórica le seguirá la presentación de un breve caso clínico que ilustra la posibilidad de intervención utilizando este paradigma.

Conceptos clave: auto-regulación, cara immóvil, regulación interactiva, estado de conciencia diádica

L'espressione di un antico bisogno di compagnia: Infant research e analisi bioenergetica (Italian)

Il presente articolo intende affrontare il tema del dialogo tra l'analisi bioenergetica e l'infant research. Nel farlo verrà presentato il paradigma della "still face" che permette di esplorare i processi di autoregolazione, di regolazione interattiva, e la radice corporea della regolazione emotiva mostrando come l'autrice ha usufruito dei risultati della ricerca scientifica per arricchire il suo patrimonio formativo e clinico bioenergetico. Un esempio di integrazione che può essere seguito poiché ne vengono illustrati gli aspetti teorici e pratici. Verrà anche presentato un breve caso clinico che esemplifica una possibilità di intervento utilizzando questo paradigma.

Parole chiave: autoregolazione, paradigma della Still-Face, regolazione interattiva, stato diadico di coscienza

A expressão da necessidade tardia de companhia: pesquisa infantil e Análise Bioenergética (Portuguese)

Este artigo visa examinar o diálogo entre análise bioenergética e pesquisa infantil. O paradigma *still-face* é introduzido, permitindo a exploração de processos de auto-regulação e regulação interativa, bem como a origem corporal da regulação emocional. Ao examinar o paradigma *still-face*, a autora mostra como usou os resultados de pesquisas científicas para enriquecer seus recursos clínicos e didáticos no campo da Bioenergética. Este exemplo de integração é ilustrado pela apresentação de aspectos práticos e teóricos do assunto. Um pequeno estudo de caso também é apresentado, para ilustrar as possibilidades de intervenção utilizando esse paradigma.

Palavras-chave: auto-regulação, *still-face*, regulação interativa, estado diádico de consciência

The still-face paradigm

The still-face paradigm is a procedure for observing interactive behavior in infants aged between a few months and two and a half years, both in terms of normal development and in terms of evolutionary risk (Tronick, 2002; Montirosso et al., 2008). The validity of this procedure has been widely supported in numerous scientific studies (Mesman et al., 2009) and its main aim is to evaluate the infant's socio-emotional behavior and capacity for emotion regulation, as well as the mother's sensitiveness and responsiveness. It was developed over thirty years ago by Ed Tronick and his colleagues and is structured in three episodes of face-to-face interaction lasting two minutes each (Tronick et al., 1978). In the first episode, known as "Play", the mother is asked to interact with her child as she would usually do. In the second, known as "Still", she is asked to maintain a neutral, immobile facial expression and to refrain from interacting with the child. Finally, in the third episode, known as "Reunion", she has to go back to interacting normally with the child.

The three phases are filmed in order to have simultaneous paired images of the mother's and infant's faces, and these are subsequently analyzed frame by frame. Generally, in the Still phase, what is known as the *still-face effect* can be observed: the infant shows discomfort, which is expressed through negative emotions, motor agitation or, less frequently, stillness similar to that of the mother. In addition to these behaviors, other significant bodily signs are recorded, including a decrease in glances toward the mother and an increase in visual scanning and in the number of requests to be picked up (Adamson et al., 2003; Toda et al., 1993; Weinberg et al., 1999). Faced with his mother's continued unavailability for interaction, the infant feels forced to employ strategies aimed at self-regulating his negative emotional state resulting from a situation which, in some respects, could be seen as similar to the depressive response of self-absorption that some mothers may manifest (Tronick et al., 1978; Carter et al., 1990). In this sense, the still-face paradigm is an opportunity to evaluate the type of behavior the infant employs in order to regulate his own emotional state and/or how he tries to re-establish the normal interactive pattern by involving the adult as the external regulator of his emotions. We can often observe, on the part of the infant, self-comforting and self-stimulating gestures such as sucking and manipulating parts of his own body, or even freezing behaviors such as the immobilization of body language and gestures.

The interruption of communication with the mother is a particular condition that demonstrates how much young infants "expect" to interact with another human being and how the desire for company is one of the primary motivations for movement, with signals of calling out – such as crying – or more-active behaviors such as visual scanning and rotation of the head. If this searching is unsuccessful – if this reaching out toward the world doesn't meet with a response – infants find themselves in a situation of destruction and impoverishment in terms of their relationship, which is reminiscent of the image described by Alexander Lowen regarding the development of the schizoid or oral character types. The discomfort resulting from the stillness of the mother's face is so significant that three-month-old babies manifest greater stress and gaze avoidance during the phase of maternal inexpressiveness than during short periods of separation from their parent (Field, 1994).

Even though this paradigm is artificial, it nevertheless enables us to have a very real idea of what happens during maternal unavailability and during the early organization of methods of self-regulation and interactive regulation. It shows the central role of the processes of repair when faced with the fact that the mother's attention, previously mainly oriented towards evaluating the capacity for attunement, is now detached from involvement in real interaction.

This paradigm, as well as the repetition, in a clinical bioenergetic context, of the same relational experience through experimental work with dyads – as we shall see in the subsequent case study – enables the process of interaction, breakdown and repair to take place.

The role of repair as a metaphor for the therapeutic relationship

The still-face paradigm underlines the importance of relational capacity in repairing inevitable errors. It is the experience of the effectiveness of repair after the Still phase that structures the infant's trust in himself and in the relationship. Research carried out by Tronick and his colleagues (2008) shows that, in real interaction, the mother and infant spend 70 to 80 percent of the time in a state of non-harmony without this being an indicator of dysfunction in the relationship itself. The health of the relationship is measured not so much by the time spent in harmony, but rather by the dyad's capacity for good repair in an appropriate amount of time.

What's more, from a clinical point of view we know that excessive attunement can, in fact, lie at the root of the development of narcissistic discomfort (Sander 2007). It becomes evident that the fundamental point is for the dyad to manage to repair the error. In this sense it is a method for exploring in a realistic way the relational breakdowns that take place every day in the mother-infant relationship – and in every other relationship, including therapeutic ones. It is the dynamics of this process (of interaction, breakdown and repair in terms of communication and relationships) that enable us to introject a representation of the Self with the capacity to transform negative emotional states into positive states. When this happens, what we experience – whatever our age – is a sensation of being in control of ourselves, that wonderful sensation of self-possession which, for Lowen, is one of the three pillars in the development of the embodied Self (Lowen, 1994).

Next to this trust in himself and through successful situations of repair, the infant develops that relational trust, which he can channel towards a calm and solid bond of attachment. The experience of repair underlies the construction of such a bond in adult relationships, too. In this case the breakdown is the moment when we express our discomfort and the repair is the moment when we feel that the other person has understood our experience and both parties come out of the situation enriched and strengthened.

On the other hand, experiencing repeated breakdowns in communication with partial and/or inappropriate repair makes an infant build a negative emotional nucleus characterized by anger and sadness and by a process of withdrawing from dealings with the world. To put it in bioenergetic terms, he becomes involved in building methods of withdrawal or avoidance with tensions or areas of breakdown – that include the eye area, the arms and the general level of activation – which lead to situations of hyperactivation or states of disassociation. This withdrawal, which is accompanied by denied or hidden feelings, is often expressed by a relatively significant lack of awareness. On countless occasions, our patients tell stories of their relationship failures but remain unaware of their own contribution to the failure, which lies in the reactivation of old interactive methods. Such an understanding cannot happen without a person becoming open to the reciprocal processes of emotion regulation.

The movement of opening and reaching out toward the world and the movement of withdrawal are central aspects in bioenergetics regarding the organization of character, or, if we prefer, the organization of personality.

These movements are reminiscent of the amoebae studied by Wilhelm Reich, which exhibit movements of expansion in the presence of a favorable environment and of withdrawal in the presence of adverse conditions. When an infant is forced to resort to forms of self-regulation for a prolonged period of time, or when his reaching out encounters unfavorable environmental conditions, his nascent relational capacity can be compromised (Tronick, 1989; Tronick et al., 1986).

Processes of self-regulation, since they are not expressions of withdrawal, need to be integrated with processes of interactive regulation. Reaching out and withdrawing should be fluid and vibrant movements, as, indeed, all movements should be. Offering adult patients in a clinic the possibility to experiment with, and not simply talk about, the experience of breakdown and repair enables us to understand, through the body, our relational method, thus making bioenergetic work a real somatic-relational process (Seick, 2007). In this work, as Louis Sander states, "We are not looking for the past, but for the logic of the strategies for regulating a patient's internal states" (in Schwaber, 1990, p. 228).

In general we continue to have recourse to interactive regulation, both for the pleasure of and the need for company and in the search for external help when the task we face is greater than our capacities. This is exactly what infants do. Moreover, in addition to this, co-regulation allows an infant to increase the capacity of his system, which is still immature.

We are driven toward therapeutic relationships by the need for interactive regulation, the expression of that age-old desire for company and the need to repair an *unresolved error*, which is an instance of *interactive regulation* that did not work properly and has left a mark on the pattern of self-regulation. The result of the repair will provide the meaning of the experience as a whole: interaction, lack of harmony, breakdown and repair. The experience of lack of harmony, which is so realistic in life, does not have a negative meaning in itself: it enables the infant to deal with new, expanding developmental tasks, just as it enables the patient to find new meanings for his own existence.

In this case, attention shifts from the trauma – the absence of communication in the *still* phase – to the relational process as a whole and the capacity of the dyad to repair the failure by expanding its own world of meanings in this way and allowing the growth and development of new and more complex methods of living in the world. Through these processes many of the subjective meanings, which settle in the personal memory and the emotional and physical biography of each individual, are built. Lowen anticipated this sensitivity and used it in his clinical work with adult patients: "The individual, who as a child or infant had never consciously experienced certain sensations, cannot acquire them through analysis. Where a person has suffered from a lack of feelings of security in early life, what is needed in therapy is not only analysis but the opportunity and the means to acquire that security in the present" (Lowen, 1975, p. 287).

The role of the interlocutor, caregiver or psychotherapist in the somatic-relational therapeutic process is to offer, first of all, validation to the experience that is taking place. The psychotherapist thus becomes an "empathetic co-discoverer," as David Finlay (1999) succinctly states. This validation, which is substantiated by empathetic resonance, is the sharing of a state and is not confined solely to the emotions, but also includes the state of awareness. Partaking in the understanding, which leads to repair, is a validating experience that restores self-awareness, just as the absence of self-awareness can be invalidating. At the moment in which we feel known or recognized by another, an experience of reflexive awareness begins. When the mother-infant relationship is harmonious and the caregiver understands the infant's needs and formulates a response, the experience that the infant undergoes within himself is one of increased embodied awareness, self-control and *self-agency* (Cinotti, Zaccagnini, 2009). In this sense the therapeutic process is also measured with the change, the continuity and the progressive expansion of the coherence and complexity of one's own self, a typical feature both of developmental processes and of the clinical relationship.

Methods of early regulation are also a valid indicator of how the infant will organize his own emotional experience before it becomes a stable bond of attachment (Schore 2003a, Schore 2003b). In the first six or seven months of an infant's life, we can observe an intensification of privileged contact with the mother, who is, nevertheless, not yet identified as the exclusive reference figure (Bowlby, 1969; Ainsworth et al., 1978). It is only from the second half of an infant's first year that the bond clearly emerges, fostering the development of the attachment. The quantity and quality of the interactions, breakdowns and repairs that the mother and infant undergo in the first six months represent a fundamental experience in the process of constructing the bond because they form the framework within which the type of attachment will be defined. Similarly, the first few months of psychotherapy are often the most delicate because it is during this time that an effective working partnership and a solid therapeutic relationship are being established.

Ways of being together

In fact, emotion regulation in the first few months of an infant's life follows the paths that, to a certain extent, enable us to perceive subsequent ways of "being together." Diener and his colleagues (2002) have traced some of these likely paths. The first possibility is where the infant's self-regulatory capacity and his use of interactive regulation coexist in a balanced way. The infant experiences a sense of self-efficacy or self-possession in terms of his capacity for regulating his emotions in an autonomous way and, where necessary, is flexible enough to be able to turn to an adult figure. He is able to express his own emotions – the self-expression, which forms the second pillar of the embodied Self (Lowen, 1994) – whether these are positive or negative, and the caregiver is perceived as emotionally available. The repetition of experiences of breakdown and repair and the presence of a sufficiently affectionate mother allow a fullness of self-awareness to develop, which integrates self-expression and self-possession. It is highly likely that this will be the basis for the establishment of a secure attachment.

I like to quote my colleague Silja Wendelstadt, who has spent almost thirty years studying the early mother-infant relationship through Eva Reich's gentle bioenergetic massage. In the paper she presented at a conference in Camogli, Italy, in 2009 – which was dedicated especially to "The regulation of emotions" – she discusses emotion regulation as a form of "bioenergetic contact"[1] "'Bioenergetic contact' between two human beings is a rhythmic, pulsating process, a process of tension-charge and relaxation-discharge, as Wilhelm Reich described it. All emotions have this rhythm: breastfeeding, love, joy, anger, crying and so on."

And we mustn't forget Reich himself, who states in "Children of the

1 My collaboration with Rosario Montirosso, an Italian researcher who works very closely with Ed Tronick, has produced two educational events: a conference entitled "La regolazione emotiva" ("Emotion regulation") in Camogli in 2009 and two seminars for advanced-level study: "Gli affetti come organizzatori dell'esperienza" ("Emotions as organisers of experience"), in Genoa in 2010, led by Rosario Montirosso, and "La regolazione delle emozioni nella relazione precoce madre-bambino" ("The regulation of emotions in the early mother-infant relationship"), led by myself and Rosario Montirosso.

Future": "The bioenergetic sense of contact, a function of the energy field of both the mother and the child, is unknown to specialists. Bioenergetic contact is the most essential experiential and emotional element in the interrelationship between mother and child, particularly prenatally and during the first days and weeks of life. On it, basically, the future fate of the child depends. It seems to be the core of the emotional development of the newborn infant. We know very little about it" (Reich, 1942).

It seems that both of them are speaking, using different words, about that process of mutual reciprocal regulation that concerns us[2] (Tronick, 2008).

If emotion regulation is focused solely on self-directed methods – in other words on self-consolation, self-stimulation and the exploration of one's environment in order to limit the need to turn to an adult – we will also find linked to this a reduced expression of negative emotions and the mitigation of positive ones. That's because the adult reference figure is identified right away as not available to provide relief from negative emotions. Such a condition can easily develop into an avoidant attachment bond. The capacity for protesting through frustration is inhibited or excessively mitigated.

Tronick (2008) repeatedly underlines how incapacity for coherent protest is transformed into restrained and inhibited behavior. From a bioenergetic point of view, it is inevitable there be a reference to the important role taken on by actions that "organize" protest, such as kicking and hitting, accompanied by the word "No," the manifestation of a breakdown that could not be expressed either through anger or through sadness. Helping the patient to reorganize this "aborted" behavior can restore that sense of self-control, which he has probably lost.

2 The Mutual Recognition Model (MRM) (Tronick, 1989) aims to define the socio-emotional processes of communication microregulation that produce the unique and specific characteristics of the relationship in question. The simultaneous communication of the affective evaluation of what is happening in the interaction between mother and infant creates, or rather co-creates, relational movements which go from phases of forward movement (moving along) through "now moments" to "moments of meeting" (Stern, 1998). The attention to co-creation underlines the dynamic and unpredictable aspects present in the mother-infant relationship, just as in any other relationship. Ed Tronick prefers the term "co-create" to "co-construct", which is more typical of Stern, to underline that there is no definite final state to be reached (for example secure attachment), rather a continuous becoming of affective movements. An important consequence of co-creativity is that interactive "defects", instead of indicating something that is not working in the interaction, form the material for co-creating new ways of being together. For further exploration of the subject, see Tronick, 2008.

A third outcome, finally, is that the infant resorts exclusively to regulation by another. In such a case, when experiencing discomfort, he will search excessively for relational support and will display a tendency for hyperactivity. In this case the infant emphasizes the expression of negative emotions to attract the attention of the caregiver, who often adopts intrusive relational methods with a low degree of predictability or, conversely, with a constant tendency towards emotional unavailability, often developing an ambivalent-resistant attachment (Fedeli et al., 2010). These infants grow into patients who remain passive, waiting for therapy to provide a solution to the problem. They need to find their own roots and their own ground in order to grasp the sense of their own personal and relational movement. These patients need to learn to experience their own company, instead of always relying on "the other", whose presence as emotional regulator is all-powerful in their lives.

Regulation of emotions is not only concerned with short-term emotional states, but also with ones that are more prolonged and those that play a part in the structure of the infant's mood. Tronick (2002) suggests this takes shape like an emotional process that plays an anticipatory role with regard to future experiences. On a related note, Daniel Stern talks about the *vitality profile*, meaning the rhythm, timing, form and intensity of the communicative exchange within the dyad, and the expression of the temperament of both infant and mother[3].

A good example of the structuring of infant mood with regard to early relational exchanges can be observed in the case of maternal depression. Depressed mothers are less able to understand their children and, as a result, to respond in an appropriate way. They are often less empathetic and expressive, they withdraw their gaze more frequently and are more susceptible to failure during repair. As a result the infant will tend to establish a negative emotional state, thus becoming more resistant to the subsequent social stimuli he may receive. The infant, sharing his mother's sadness, will end up assimilating this and reintroducing it in his subsequent interactions with the adult (Tronick, 2005).

It is no coincidence that infants with depressed mothers tend not to look

3 In clinical bioenergetics, Guy Tonella has explored this aspect, making a distinction between emotions, understood as emotive events, and vitality profiles (Sander 2007; Stern 1985, Tronick 2008): if emotions are, by their very nature, transitory, vitality profiles constitute stable methods of activation which people experience and tolerate, the expression of their energetic profile, to use a phrase that was very dear to Lowen.

at their own mother, to display prolonged negative feelings and generally to come across as more angry. Once it has been established, the infant's negative mood models the affective methods of "being with," compromising the quality of the socio-relational experience. The interactive methods adopted early on by the mother tend to become established over time and have an effect on the quality of the infant's behavioral, cognitive and socio-relational development (Murray and Cooper, 1997). The children of depressed mothers display more negative interaction with unfamiliar adults, are less competent on a social level and interact less (Field, 1998). These are infants who have a significant effect on people from outside the family. Even when these outsiders are unfamiliar with the infant's story, they tend to smile less, have less physical contact with the infant and keep a greater interpersonal distance. This is exactly what happens with depressed patients, who tend to withdraw their gaze and have a lower motor activity level, and who risk receiving less suitable treatment.

The methods of interaction used by depressed mothers do not all form a homogeneous whole. At least two types of interactive pattern have been identified. On the one hand, there are mothers who employ more-intrusive relational methods and on the other, by contrast, there are mothers with a marked tendency towards detachment and withdrawal. The children of hostile and intrusive mothers are faced with a different emotional climate from the children of detached and withdrawn mothers. In the first case, the mothers tend to interrupt the infant's activities and even prevent interactions being repaired. Faced with an obstacle to his activities, the infant experiences a state of anger, which, if repeated, will become internalized. By contrast, in the case of detached or withdrawn mothers, infants display regulation characterized by self-comfort, and the repetition of relational failure will foster the development of a mood characterized by sadness.

Supervision in the light of emotion regulation

An analysis of the intrinsic developmental processes in the mother-infant relationship allows us easily to grasp some of the dynamics between patient and therapist, thus helping us to understand what brings about therapeutic change. It is precisely because of its predominantly non-verbal aspects that mother-infant interaction presents itself as a powerful model for investigating that "extra something" that "happens" in every relationship characterized by strong emotional involvement, like the therapeutic relationship.

In the three years of supervision in the light of emotion regulation, which I have run with a group of bioenergetic colleagues, analysis of the therapeutic *error* was preceded by analysis of the repair of the error, which the therapist carried out, often unconsciously and on a bodily and non-verbal level, immediately after producing the breakdown. Concentrating on this has given us a better understanding both of the colleague's style of repair and of those elements of bodily resonance that led him to tune in to the most-suitable kind of repair for that particular moment. Attention to self-regulatory processes of repairing breakdown also allow us to evaluate how much the therapeutic relationship is moving toward new ways of responding with regard to attachment figures and how much past experiences continue to be repeated.

This perspective is interesting because it overturns the subject previously being explored in supervision and allows us to minimize the aspects of shame and guilt linked to the error and place greater value on aspects of resourcefulness, which are so important to the therapeutic relationship.

Supervision in the light of emotion regulation is a two-person process. Patient and therapist are involved in a reciprocal system of development, which is mediated by perception, exploration and awareness of emotions. Like the mother-infant dyad, they use subtle bodily indicators, and supervision increases awareness of these. In this sense, the patient and therapist are involved in a system of mutual reciprocal regulation that Tronick discusses with regard to the mother-infant relationship. In this process of supervision, self-regulation becomes a tool for understanding the bodily organization of defenses, while interactive regulation enables us to grasp how the patient-psychotherapist dyad moves, opening a new, interesting chapter concerning *relational movements.*

Therapeutic change: relational movements

We cannot forget that underlying vegetotherapy and bioenergetic analysis is the understanding that movement is the language of the body as it expresses an emotion, or the way in which we organize ourselves in order to hold back an emotion (Reich, 1933; Lowen, 1958). We cannot, however, confine ourselves solely to reading the body if we really want to lay claim to the somatic-relational nature of current bioenergetic analysis. Therefore, in the light of emotion regulation, the patient-therapist dyad is also involved in a relational movement of reciprocal microregulation, which we discussed a short time ago, and in a proper relational movement of more macroscopic dimensions.

With regard to this, Stern (1971, 1985, 1998, Stern et. al. 1985) talks about three relational movements: *moving along*, which represents the phase of forward movement, and *now moment* and *moment of meeting*, which are the expression of the space-time in which the transforming meeting takes place. This space-time is always the present (Stern, 2004). The present is when the corrective emotional experience comes about, and is linked to experiencing something new. This new experience redefines the relational model and allows the phase of forward movement, of integration of the traumatic experience and of newness to come about, transforming the experience that is taking place.

In this case, the reading of relational movements in the supervision process also strengthens the aspects of bodily resonance that are very closely linked to bioenergetic practice and provides a perspective less oriented towards failure and more oriented towards the therapeutic process. It's a process where the patient and therapist experiment with new relational movements or update old methods of response, which are also an expression of their methods of self-regulation.

Beatrice Beebe and Frank Lachmann (2002) have emphasized the role of bi-directional coordination as an essential element for understanding the processes of co-construction of meaning, which are typical in each human relationship. Although every individual can be conceived of as a self-regulating unit, it is similarly evident that processes of regulation by another do not only organize behavior but also design the sense of relational experience and first-person lived experience. The dyad – whether it is parent and infant or therapist and patient – moves within an interactive matrix, which provides the frame of meaning for lived experience.

It is no coincidence that Tronick talks about "dyadic expansion of consciousness." If there is adequate emotion regulation in the mother-infant system, it becomes possible to tackle, resolve and incorporate increasingly complex tasks. Through these acquisitions the infant expands his own state of consciousness of the world, becoming more complex and coherent. The same thing happens in the therapeutic relationship, which provides the patient – through the experience of a different, interactive regulation – the opportunity to acquire a more-effective self-regulation that is better adapted to the situation. The emergence of a dyadic state of consciousness allows us to move forward in terms of mental organization since it creatively provides new "scenarios" of being together.

A short clinical case

Maria is a patient whom I have been treating for four years. When she began treatment, she had a serious phobic disturbance that caused her to have paranoid thoughts toward strangers, whom she perceived as criminals. It also made her develop a severe eating disorder based on the idea that certain foods were polluted or contaminated. Within six months she had lost more than ten kilos (twenty pounds). Her fear prevented her from having any pharmacological treatments, including those involving psychopharmacological drugs, which would have been very useful when she began treatment. Despite the severity of her symptoms, she appeared normal and successfully hid her phobia of contact by using ingenious tricks. Her situation had deteriorated considerably and was serious enough to force her to ask for help because of a problem at work. She feared she was becoming insane and, even worse, was afraid that other people would notice that she was dominated by her fear.

Her fear of becoming insane immediately seemed to me to be the best point of contact with reality. Maria did not believe in the reality of her thoughts, but she had to behave as if they were real. Her recognition of the distance between reality and her fears was a central point in our therapeutic partnership. We began treatment with a weekly session. After a year of individual therapy, the sessions were supplemented with a weekly bioenergetic exercise class and a monthly group session.

I am going to describe a session that took place during group work in her third year of therapy. It is an example of how I use exercises of reaching out and withdrawal as preparation for still-face work.

The initial part of the session within the group therapy works on the bow and the bend-over as tools for regulating – and self-regulating – the opening and closing of relationships. After this, I introduce dynamic grounding work to provide the opportunity of experiencing opening and withdrawal while remaining in an upright position. I use the first part as an equivalent to the interaction phase in the still-face paradigm. In fact, I prefer the person to come into contact with his own perception of himself in the opening and closing, seeing it as an expression of past relational experiences, a remembered present that allows responses to previous interactions to be brought up to date.

Then I introduce pair work where one person reaches out towards an interlocutor chosen from among the participants. The pair takes turns to have one person reaching out while the other remains immobile and non-responsive, as happens during the Still phase of the paradigm.

After this phase, I introduce work involving two movements. The first one is refusal, pushing away, using the words "away" or "enough." The second movement is reaching the arms upward and saying, "come." This gives the person the opportunity to explore – within his own bodily first-person experience – a desire for reunion as well as protest.

The third phase, that of repair, takes place in the reflective verbal working through of the experience at the end of the bodywork session. By this point Maria had acquired good embodied awareness and her fears were greatly reduced. During the discussion following the bodywork session, she related her experience very clearly: "My mother was oppressive and intrusive when she wanted to be and absent when I wanted her. When I said 'enough,' I felt like I used to feel when she came and upset me. When I said 'come,' I felt sadness for all the times when I called for her in vain."

This simple and effective description enabled Maria to formulate a better understanding of her fear: she accepted the intrusion because she was afraid of being abandoned. At the same time this intrusion was the source of "poisoning." And, parallel to this, she herself could be persecutory within her social relationships or completely unreachable, distant from contact and from the relationship.

This insight is a very small part of the therapeutic journey, but I am describing it because it clarifies very succinctly the relationship that can be structured between the body (in this case the arms), the regulation of an emotion (fear and anger) and the interactive regulation experienced with the mother. From the point of view of relational movement, my listening and understanding enabled the client to expand her awareness of her own bodily-emotional-cognitive experience. This facilitated a relational forward movement (moving along) both in the therapeutic relationship and in her confidence in her ability to distinguish what was poisoning her and how it was happening. It was an experience in which self-awareness, self-expression and self-possession helped her to integrate the past and present in a richer and fuller sense of herself and of her lived experience. Our being together and giving our shared attention to the same object, seen from two different points of view, helped her experience an intimacy far removed from the pattern of alternating intrusion and absence that she knew so well.

Sometime later, she brought me a poem, which she felt expressed very well the sense of that insight and of the still-ongoing project of working through her lived experience. The version she brought me was an Italian translation, but this is the original.

Love After Love
Derek Walcott

The time will come
when, with elation
you will greet yourself arriving
at your own door, in your own mirror
and each will smile at the other's welcome,

and say, sit here. Eat.
You will love again the stranger who was yourself.
Give wine. Give bread. Give back your heart
to itself, to the stranger who has loved you

all your life, whom you ignored
for another, who knows you by heart.
Take down the love letters from the bookshelf,

the photographs, the desperate notes,
peel your own image from the mirror.
Sit. Feast on your life.

Little by little Maria started eating again and, meal by meal, she returned to her normal weight.

Short concluding notes

As Lowen succinctly states, in words that seem as if they are dedicated to Maria: "The catalytic point of this transformation is personal experience.

The information that corresponds with our experience becomes knowledge; the rest is not assimilated, it passes through the mind and is soon forgotten" (Lowen, 1970, p. 139).

Dialogic reflection on bioenergetic analysis and infant research fits into this mold. As Tronick says: "Downing (2001) has invited the research world to reflect on the possibility that the infant develops implicit motor procedures that go along with moods. These bodily processes would be stable ways of being in a mood and expressing it. They would be ways in which we, as well as others, come to know our moods" (Tronick, 2008, p. 273). And when speaking about future advances in research, he suggests an interpretation of the infant's dynamic internal conflicts: "In this case, this would not be (that is in the case of dynamic internal conflicts) a conflict of unconscious adult-like representational processes (which once again the infant does not yet have) but a conflict of implicit affective representational processes. It is interesting to think, following Downing (2001), that the conflict may be felt most keenly in the body" (Tronick, 2008, p. 275).

Tronick, quoting an author specialized in bioenergetic analysis training, George Downing, shows he has a clear concept of the role of bodily processes and of the fixed methods of bodily response in the processes of development.

The role of bodily resonance in bioenergetic analysis is not, however, something that is only experienced in clinical exchanges, but is what has already begun in the formative process. We can even say that it is a basic and fundamental part of the formative process. How, in fact, could we enter into resonance with our patients if our body wasn't resonant and vibrant in itself? How could we feel, in our body, the process taking place in the patient if we weren't used to being in harmony with our own bodily process? And so the body is the primary formative experience that the experience of clinical theory must follow. It is not simply an empathetic process, but it begins as a proper formative somatic-relational process. This capacity for constructing bodywork experiences in order to explore lived experience continues to be the specific, distinctive feature in an epistemological sense as well of bioenergetic analysis, and allows it to venture into other areas of clinical psychodynamics while remaining firmly anchored to its own roots.

Indeed, understanding other approaches is not tantamount to integrating a whole theoretical corpus, but means something closer to living a whole body of experience. The still-face paradigm becomes an experience that is explored after it has been employed in the expansion of embodied, emotional and cognitive awareness and in the integration of the elements that emerge. It enables us to understand the specific meaning that it has come to have in the particular story of that person and his own perceptive universe. This allows us to give solid foundations to clinical exploration, to the reconstruction of one's personal story, but also, most importantly, to the vision of the world on which the perceived present is based, integrating the clinical examination of unconscious processes with the clinical examination of conscious processes.

The foundation on which the formative process of bioenergetic analysis is based is, once again, the distinction proposed by Lowen between understanding and knowing. Formative processes are often journeys based exclusively on knowledge, on learning through study, and the key thoughts of authors concerning their own reference approach.

In bioenergetic analysis this is also the case, but there is more to it. The foundation of the formative process is in fact the understanding that comes from first-person experience, from having had a process rooted in one's own body. In this way, teacher and pupil democratically become co-constructors and co-creators of the analytic-bioenergetic culture, a creative process that is closely linked to the experience of bodywork.

References

Adamson, L. B., Frick, J. E. (2003): "The still-face: A history of a shared experimental paradigm". Infancy, 4, pp. 451–473.

Ainsworth, M. D. S., Blehar, M. C., Waters, E., Wall, S. (1978): Patterns of Attachment. A Psychological Study of the Strange Situation. Hillsdale, NJ: Erlbaum.

Beebe, B., Lachmann, F. (2002): Infant Research and Adult Treatment: Co-constructing Interactions. Hillsdale, NJ: Analytic Press.

Bowlby, J. (1969): Attaccamento e perdita. Vol.1: L'Attaccamento alla madre. It. Tr. (1972). Turin: Boringhieri.

Carter, A. S., Mayes, L. C., Pajer, K. A. (1990): "The role of dyadic affect in play and infant sex in predicting infant response to the still-face situation". Child Development, 61, pp. 764–773.

Cinotti, N., Zaccagnini, C. (eds.) (2009): Analisi bioenergetica in dialogo. Milan: Franco Angeli.

Field, T. M. (1994): "The effects of mother's physical and emotional unavailability on emotion regulation". In A. Fox (ed.), Emotion Regulation: Behavioural and Biological Considerations, Monographs of the Society for Research in Child Development, pp. 208–227. Chicago: University of Chicago Press.

Finlay, D. J. (1999): "A Relational Approach to Bioenergetics". Bioenergetic Analysis: The Clinical Journal of the International Institute for Bioenergetic Analysis, 10, 2.

Lowen, A. (1958, 1971): Physical Dynamics of Character Structure. New York: Grune & Stratton. Italian translation (1978): Il linguaggio del corpo. Milan: Feltrinelli.

Lowen, A. (1970): Pleasure. New York: Penguin Books. Italian translation (1984): Il piacere. Rome: Astrolabio.

Lowen, A. (1975): Bioenergetics. New York: Coward. Italian translation (1983): Bioenergetica. Milan: Feltrinelli.

Lowen, A. (1994): Joy: The Surrender to the Body. Italian translation (1994): Arrendersi al corpo. Rome: Astrolabio.

Mesman, J., van Ijzendoorn, M.H., Bakermans-Kranenburg, M.J. (2009): "The many faces of the still-face paradigm: A review and meta-analysis". Developmental Review, 29, pp. 120–162.

Montirosso, R., Tronick, E.Z. (2008): "Comportamento socio-emozionale della madre e del bambino di 30 mesi e caratteristiche interattive della diade durante una versione modificata del paradigma still-face". In Riva Crugnola, C., and Rodini, C. (eds.), Regolazione emotiva. Raffaello Cortina Editore.

Reich, W. (1934): Charakteranalyse. New York: Orgone Institute Press. Italian translation (1975): Analisi del carattere. Milan: Sugarco.

Reich, W. (1942): The Function of the Orgasm. New York: Orgone Institute Press. Italian translation (1975): La funzione dell'orgasmo. Milan: Sugarco.

Reich, W. (1942): Children of the Future. New York: Orgone Institute Press. Italian translation (1987): Bambini del futuro. Milan: Sugarco.

Sander, L. (2007) Sistemi viventi. Milan: Cortina.

Schore, A. N. (2003a): Affect Dysregulation and the Disorders of the Self. New York: Norton & Co.

Schore, A. N. (2003b): Affect Regulation and the Repair of the Self. New York: Norton & Co. Italian translation (2008): La regolazione degli affetti e la riparazione del sé. Rome: Astrolabio.

Stern, D. (1971): "A microanalysis of mother-infant interaction". Journal of the American Academy of Child Psychiatry, 19, pp. 501–517. It. tr.(1998) in Stern, D., Le interazioni madre-bambino. Milan: Cortina.

Stern, D., Hofer, L., Haft, W., Dore, J. (1985): "Affect attunement: the sharing of feeling states between mother and infant by means of intermodal fluency" in Field, T., Fox, N (eds.), Social Perception in Infants. Norwood, NJ: Able. Italian translation (1998) in Stern, D., Le interazioni madre-bambino. Milan: Cortina.

Stern, D. N. (1985): The Interpersonal World of the Infant. New York: Basic Books. Italian translation (1987): Il mondo interpersonale del bambino. Turin: Bollati Boringhieri.

Stern, D. N. (1989): "La rappresentazione dei modelli di relazione: considerazioni evolutive" in Sameroff, A. J., Emde, R. N. (1989): Relationships Disturbances in Early Childhood. A Developmental Approach. New York: Basic Books. Italian translation (1991): I disturbi delle relazioni nella prima infanzia. Turin: Bollati Boringhieri.

Stern, D. N. et al. (1998): "Non-interpretive Mechanisms in Psychoanalytic Therapy" in International Journal of Psychoanalysis, 79, 903. Italian translation (2008): Carli, L., Rodini, C. (eds.), Le forme di intersoggettività. Milan: Cortina.

Stern, D. N. (2000): "Putting time back into our considerations of infant experience: a microdiachronic view". Infant Mental Health Journal, vol.21 (1–2), pp. 21–28.

Stern, D. N. (2004): The Present Moment in Psychotherapy and Everyday Life. New York: Norton. Italian translation (2005): Il momento presente in psicoterapia e nella vita quotidiana. Milan: Cortina.

Toda, S., Fogel, A. (1993): "Infant response to the still-face situation at 3 and 6 months". Developmental Psychology, 29, pp. 532–538.
Tronick, E.Z., Als, H., Adamson, L.B., Wise, S., Brazelton, T.B. (1978): "The infant's response to entrapment between contradictory messages in face-to-face interaction". Journal of the American Academy of Child Psychiatry, 17, pp. 1–13.
Tronick, E.Z., Gianino, A. (1986): "Interactive mismatch and repair: Challenges to the copy infant". Zero to Three: Bulletin of the National Center for Clinical Infant Programs, 5, pp. 1–6.
Tronick, E.Z. (1989): "Emotion and emotional communication in infants". American Psychologist, 44, pp. 112–119.
Tronick, E.Z. (2002): The Neurobehavioral and Social-Emotional Development of Infants and Children. New York: Norton & Company.
Weinberg, M.K., Tronick, E.Z. (1996): "Infant affective reactions to the resumption of maternal interaction after the still-face". Child Development, 65, pp. 905–914.
Weinberg, M.K., Tronick, E.Z., Cohn, J.F., Olson, K.L. (1999): "Gender differences in emotional expressivity and self-regulation during early infancy". Developmental Psychology, 35, pp. 175–188.

About the Author

Nicoletta Cinotti, Psychologist, Psychotherapist, Italian Bioenergetic Analyst, CBT Supervisor (Siab) and teacher on the SIAB course for counsellors in body mediation and on the SIAB training course for psychotherapists. She is interested in regulation of emotion in body psychotherapy and how to work to integrate self-regulation and interactive regulation in body psychotherapy and bioenergetic analysis. She wrote several publications on bioenergetic analysis. She works with Clinical activity as a psychotherapist, treating individuals, groups and couples in Genoa and Chiavari and provides residential psychotherapy seminars. E-mail: nicoletta.cinotti@gmail.com.

Neurobiological Theory and Models

A Help or Hindrance in the Clinical Encounter?

Robert Lewis

Abstracts

English

This paper examines the clinical relevance of recent neuroscience data to the practice of bioenergetic analysis. I conclude that the nonverbal, bodily basis of our approach is affirmed by the evolving picture of a right-brain-to right-brain infant-caregiver dialogue engraving our attachment experience into the right limbic system as a model of relationships to come. But I also conclude that, for most of us, the neurobiological data does not help us in real time to be present with our patient in the clinical encounter. Two clinical vignettes illustrate both the above perspective and the continuing relevance of our basic Reichian/Lowenian model of our patient as the trillion-celled amoeba.

Key words: neurobiology, relational, mirroring, intuitive, paradigm

Neurobiologische Daten: Eine Hilfe oder ein Hindernis in der klinischen Begegnung? (German)

Dieser Vortrag prüft die klinische Bedeutung der neuen neurobiologischen Daten für die Praxis der bioenergetischen Analyse. Ich komme zu dem Schluss, dass die nonverbale Körpergrundlage unseres Ansatzes bestätigt wird durch das sich entwickelnde Bild eines Dialoges der rechten zur rechten Gehirnhälfte zwischen Säugling und Bezugsperson. Dieses Zwiegespräch prägt unsere Bindungserfahrung in das rechte limbische System ein als ein Modell für kommende Beziehungen. Ich komme aber auch zu dem Schluss, dass den meisten unter uns die neurobiologischen Daten in Echtzeit nicht helfen in der klinischen Begegnung gegenwärtig zu sein mit unserem Patienten. Zwei klinische Beispiele demonstrieren beides, die obige Perspektive und die andauernde Bedeutung unseres Reich/Lowen-Grundmodells unseres Patienten als eine aus Billionen Zellen Bestehende.

Schlüsselwörter: Neurobiologie: relational, Spiegelung: intuitiv, Paradigma

Données Neurobiologiques: Une Aide ou un Obstacle dans la Rencontre Clinique? (French)

Cet article étudie la pertinence clinique des données récentes de neuroscience à la pratique de l'Analyse Bioénergétique. Je conclus que la base corporelle non verbale de notre approche est confirmée par l'image d'un dialogue du cerveau droit de l'enfant au cerveau droit du donneur de soin se développant et gravant leur expérience d'attachement dans le système limbique droit comme un modèle de relation à venir. Mais je conclus aussi que, pour la plupart d'entre nous, les données biologiques ne nous aident pas dans le temps présent réel à être présent avec notre patient dans la rencontre clinique. Les deux vignettes cliniques illustrent à la fois la perspective ci-dessus et la pertinence continue de notre modèle Reichien/Lowenien de notre patient comme l'amibe au milliard de milliard de cellules.

Mots Clés: neuroscience, cerveau droit, limbique, Reich, Lowen

Modelos y Teoría Neurobiológica: Una Ayuda o una Dificultad en el Encuentro Clínico? (Spanish)

Este artículo examina la relevancia clínica de los hallazgos neurocientíficos recientes para la práctica del análisis bioenergético. Concluyo que la base no verbal, corporal de nuestro enfoque queda afirmada por la imagen cambiante de un diálogo de cerebro derecho-a-cerebro derecho entre el niño y el cuidador, que graba nuestra experiencia de apego en el sistema límbico como un modelo futuro de relaciones. Pero también concluyo que, para la mayoría de nosotros, los datos neurobiológicos no nos ayudan en tiempo real a estar presentes con nuestro paciente en el encuentro clínico. Dos ejemplos clínicos ilustran la perspectiva antes mencionada y la continua relevancia de nuestro modelo Reichiano/Loweniano básico de nuestro paciente como la ameba con trillones de células.

Conceptos clave: relacional, reflejar, intuitivo, paradigma

Teoria e modelli neurobiolologici: un aiuto o un impedimento nell'incontro clinico? (Italian)

Questo scritto esamina la rilevanza clinica delle recenti scoperte neuroscentifiche per la prassi dell'analisi bioenergetica. Giungo alla conclusione che la base corporea non verbale del nostro approccio è confermata dal quadro del dialogo tra i cervelli destri del care-giver e del bambino che incide sulla nostra esperienza di attaccamento nel sistema limbico destro in quanto modello di relazione. Ma concludo anche che, per molti di noi, i dati neurobiologici non sono di aiuto per essere presenti in tempo reale nell'incontro clinico con i nostri pazienti. Due vignette cliniche illustrano quanto già affermato e la perdurante rilevanza del nostro modello reichiano/loweniano di base dei nostri pazienti che possiamo considerare amebe con miliardi di cellule.

Parole chiave: neurobiologia, relazionale, rispecchiamento, intuitive, paradigma

Aporte neurobiológico: Ajuda ou Obstáculo no Encontro Clínico? (Portuguese)

Este artigo examina a relevância clínica de recentes dados da neurociência para a prática da Análise Bioenergética. Concluo que a base corporal para nossa abordagem reside no processo evolutivo do diálogo cérebro-direito-para-cérebro-direito do bebê com o cuidador, gravando nossa experiência de apego no sistema límbico direito, como modelo de futuros relacionamentos. Mas, concluo também que, para a maioria de nós, os dados neurobiológicos não ajudam a estar presente com nosso paciente, em tempo real, no encontro clínico. Duas vinhetas clínicas ilustram tanto a perspectiva citada acima como a contínua relevância do nosso modelo Reicheano/Loweniano básico do paciente como a ameba de trilhões de células.

Palavras-chave: neurociência, cérebro direito, límbico, Reich, Lowen

Introduction[1]

This paper concerns the clinical relevance and implications of recent neuroscience research ... that is, new data about the mind/brain/body continuum. Not surprisingly, perhaps obviously, my overall message will be that the relevance of these discoveries resides in and depends on who *you*, the therapist are, who the patient is, and what's happening or not happening in the therapy process between the two of you.

So, I will be examining what Neurobiology can and cannot do for the clinical craft of conducting Bioenergetic therapy. I will also consider whether we are moving toward a new paradigm along the mind/brain/body continuum, and will touch on a few related clinical issues. Implied in all this, is the practical question: will neurobiology change our Bioenergtic curriculum and the way we teach our craft?

We need all the help we can get in our chosen profession as wounded healers. We are sorely tested when our work is with patients whose grief, abuse and other traumatic experiences have broken their connection with their essential value as human beings ... whose wounds, in other words, resonate with our own. Often, because we earn our livelihood from this work, many of us do not (I know I do not) often sufficiently reduce our fees so that our patients can see us as often as would be optimal for them. We ask these patients to face the dark night of their souls, even though they are actually often only with us for a single session during a week's time. So we need all the help we can get to both be with them in the shame of their raw, inchoate brokenness and in the beauty and grace of self that is deeply interwoven with that woundedness.

A theory or model is a kind of story, and we all develop stories that explain our interventions, both to our patients and ourselves. In line with our

1 In this paper I will use the masculine personal pronoun for purposes of simplicity.

conference theme[2], these stories may incorporate data from neuroscience, just as they have done with Reichian/Lowenian models or the Attachment paradigm. These stories often give us more faith, as therapists, in what we are doing, because we feel our interventions are supported by "science". If, for instance, you are a predominantly left-brained, top-down kind of therapist, neuro-imaging gives you a left-brained way of understanding that your attuned, attentive right –hemispheric response to your patient is building balance and integration into his psyche-soma.

However, state of the art fMRI studies are of healthy volunteers lying in a huge machine. When the brains of these volunteers respond empathically to something they view via high-tech goggles, inferences are made as to what might be going on generically in the brain between people or in an actual therapy situation! The overarching principle here is that, as always, the stories we tell and the way we embody them in the room with our patients, has a relational/transference/counter-transference significance to our patient. In this sense, I do not believe that clinical neurobiological constructs are exempt from a general truth about clinical theory: that our patient will be moved towards a more secure and balanced self, to the extent that it, the theory or construct, helps us, the therapist, to be the kind of person that was lacking in our patient's family of origin: someone attuned to the body and mind of the other, someone who cares deeply about the patient's subjective inner experience, even while respecting that he can never fully know it.

In summary, like Margit Koemeda (2011), I have been both impressed with recent discoveries in neurobiology and yet convinced that they do not inform us how, in real time, to better practice the craft of being a Bioenergetic therapist. Having said this, many of us **are** helped by this new information.

Head, Brain, Body – a Paradigm Shift?

Neuro-biologically informed clinicians and researchers are in a well-established tradition, that builds on the unity and duality of psyche – soma, on which bioenergetics is based. Alan Schore, Joachim Bauer, Daniel

2 This paper was adapted from a keynote presentation at the October 2011 IIBA conference held in San Diego, California

Siegel, Marco Iacoboni, Robert Scaer, and many others in recent decades have been filling in Reich's equation with incredible detail – down to the subunits of the genes as they interact with our experiences. But the mind/brain/body continuum, with which they are concerned, represents, in my opinion, a major shift in emphasis – perhaps even a paradigm shift – from that of classical Bioenergetics. The shift I am talking about is from the centrality of the body, to its getting no more than co-equal billing with the mind/brain/head. As you know, in classical Bioenergetics, the head/brain/mind were seen as blocking our deeper, more vital experience, and the therapy was structured to get one out of the head and into the body. Now I *do* realize that the head is part of the body, and some of you may know that I have been urging it's integration with the rest of the body for about 35 years. Actually, I did this while Al Lowen was still at the helm of our ship, and on several occasions he let me know that I was straying a bit too far. In support of this changed perspective, I quote my colleague Helen Resneck-Sannes. In her 2007 IIBA Journal article, "the Embodied Mind", she quotes Kathy Butler:

> "No longer is the skull a black box, its clockwork invisible as it was to Sigmund Freud, Carl Jung, Reich (Helen adds, Lowen) and the seminal thinkers and clinicians who have shaped 20th-century psychotherapy …"(2005) (p. 39, IIBA, 2007(17).

Now Helen and I mostly agree, but we also have a tantalizing way of not quite being on the same page. Helen continues and I quote:

> "As Bioenergetic analysts, we talk about being body therapists and learn the various muscles and their functions. However, we leave off the head, as if it isn't part of the body" (p. 40).

To the extent that Helen is accurate here, then our choosing our conference theme of integrating brain/mind and body would indeed represent a full-fledged paradigm shift. But as I said a few minutes ago, I have for many years been writing about and teaching and practicing the view that many of us choose a body-oriented therapy, precisely because we live in our armored, dissociated heads, which we do not experience as part of our bodies, and this condition dissociates us from the vitality of our bodies from the neck down. I call this condition cephalic shock (1976), and it is the somatic correlate (1984) of what Donald Winnicott (1960) called the mind as the locus of the false self. A more current name for my construct might be "cephalic freeze immobility response". While I have not yet tried the amygdala maneuver that Helen employs later in her same article, I have long worked to help my patients experience their heads as part of their flesh and blood (living) body, and thereby reduce their driven mentation or compulsive thinking, and even find some peace of mind. Neither Winnicott nor I, when I first described the clinical construct of cephalic shock in 1975, had the benefit of fMRI technology, and our clinical constructs clearly lack the specificity of the correlations of various functions with activity in specific areas of the brain. I was heartened to hear from her vignette,[3] that Dr. Koemeda was moved to engage her patient's head as a crucial entry into a healing rebirthing experience. *I do hope* that well into our post-Lowenian era, many Bioenergetic Analysts have been including the head as part of the body, even before showing up for this conference.

In summary, I suggested that in 1976 I initiated a paradigm shift within bioenergetics, a shift that included the head and mind/brain within it as co-equal in importance to the trillion-celled pulsatile amoeba that we are. I consider this my most important contribution to Bioenergetic analysis: an alternative explanation to that of Reich for the mind/body dissociation. I proposed, as did Winnicott, that the reason people are not able to experience the vitality of their bodies is precisely because they are trapped in a dissociated cerebral fortress, in which they are holding onto themselves for dear life against a fear of insanity/falling forever. This head (fortress) cannot be gotten out of. It must be gotten into, via encountering the "unthinkable anxieties" (Winnicott, 1962. P. 57–58) that are held within it. Standing our classical paradigm on its head is disorienting, so many of my colleagues may not grasp (let alone agree with) how substantially different a view of somato-psychic integration and dissociation is represented by my clinical construct of cephalic shock.

How Does Neurobiology Help Us?

As I have said, we all need explicit and/or implicit theories or models and related interventions to help us in this impossible profession. Those of us who came to the healing profession with more than our share of wound-

3 This vignette was part of Margit Koemeda's keynote at the October, 2011 IIBA conference. Her keynote, including the vignette, also appears in this volume of *Bioenergetic Analysis*.

ing and despair, cannot afford to underestimate the importance of whatever sustains our hope – the hope, I might add, that will then resonate in our patients. Many of us who as children were not attuned to by our parents, carry a deep wound regarding the value of our deeper self. When we now try to offer the empathy and compassion that we were not given, and our difficult patient does not respond positively, our doubts about the real worth of the person we are often surface. How fortunate are we that Allan Schore, for instance, teaches us that these amazing neuro-images demonstrate that our simple kindness and attunement are quietly brain changing.

Let me give you a personal example of the use or misuse of one of these models. I don't know how many of you know that I used to be a bad copy both of Al Lowen and myself (there are no good copies, by the way). For the first 5 or 10 years of my Bioenergetic career I kept my self and my patients busy. I filled my thoughts with characterological schemas and interacted with the patients around Bioenergetic techniques and exercises, so that I would not feel my fear of the intimacy of being in the same room with another human being. In this sense I used the classical Bioenergetic model quite like a therapist would use self-touch, to soothe himself and regulate his arousal and feelings. In spite of this horrific description, I believe that some of my patients were well served both because of the inherent efficacy of the Bioenergetic interventions, and because my Bioenergetic armamentarium provided me with scaffolding from which I felt safe enough for something healing in me to come forth to my patients.

As time went by, I myself felt that my Bioenergtic approach was deeply validated by the attachment paradigm, and especially the work of mother-infant observers such as Karlen Lyons-Ruth and Beatrice Beebe. First, I felt that the empiricism and inter-observer reliability of the attachment paradigm brought a solidity and respectability to the field of therapy that had been lacking. They posited classifications of infants and their parents that had good predictive ability to code for secure and insecure attachment outcomes. And then, the split-second, mutual, intuitive interactive regulation captured on mother-infant videos, spoke strongly to me of Bioenergetic analysis as an embodied relational encounter.

Neuroscience data are more empirical and objective than the data supporting many therapeutic schools or approaches. I believe they offer many of us a sense of scientific affirmation for our work, similar to what I just shared about the attachment paradigm. I think this is particularly true for us in the area of body-oriented psychotherapies, since we have been marginalized by the mainstream "talk therapies" since Ferenczi and Reich parted ways with Freud. I remember, some years back, for instance, feeling good about Allan Shore's delineation of a right-brain-to-right-brain, infant-caretaker dialogue which lays down the neural circuitry of affect regulation. The child's attachment experience, Shore proposed, has been hard-wired into his right limbic system as a model of relationships to come.

As I have said, this is a very individual matter with each of us. I had already felt affirmed by and drawn to the split-second, nonverbal communications explicated in the studies of mother-infant interaction. So, although I was intuitively drawn to Alan Shore's work, and had been fascinated by neuroanatomy from the time I was a medical student, the neuroscience data which supported Shore's model was not so important to me: I was already convinced. What we find useful from neuroscience depends on how well our existing models are working for us, and what kinds of transferences we form to the people who teach us the models, which, in turn, depends partly on how well they embody the content that they are teaching us. If we never meet them in person, it may be easier to have an idealized transference to them and their models.

Additionally, sharing knowledge about how the brain works may be helpful to some patients. Understanding something of the neural circuitry that underlies their behaviors may give the patient the necessary distance to reflect on such behaviors and thereby reduce the accompanying shame and guilt.

Also, knowledge of the brains neuroplasticity, that is the lifelong capacity of our brain cells and their connections to change, often gives hope to both therapist and patient that it is never too late.

Finally, when trying to decide how helpful some aspect of neuroscience can be for our healing, I cannot fully separate the neuroscience from its relational significance to the patient. I have developed this perspective over more than 40 years of clinical practice, and it has become deeply engrained in my neural circuitry. So, for instance, tomorrow[4] I expect you will learn about how Dan Siegel has woven aspects of neuroscience into a rich clinical method of healing that he calls mindfulness. Among the many facets of his approach, I am struck, as Dr. Siegel himself was, by the overlap between

4 This is a reference to the fact that Dan Siegel was a keynote speaker at the October 2011 IIBA Conference.

mindfulness and the processes of secure attachment. He says, "at the heart of this process, I believe, is a form of internal "tuning in" to oneself that enables people to become "their own best friend" (p. 86). So people learn how to treat themselves well, that is, they learn to tune in to themselves, from the way they are treated by Dr. Siegel. Dr. Siegel shows an exquisite sensitivity to his patient's subjective experience of their mind and body. This strikes me, as I believe it did Dr. Siegel, as a later day version of the respectfully attuned parent whose awareness of his child's inner life codes for a secure outcome. How do we distinguish the healing effect of this relational dynamic from the neuro-scientific parts of his explanatory model such as the middle prefrontal cortex, the insula and the rest of what Dr. Siegel has named the resonance circuitry? His clinical vignettes, by the way, show an extremely creative and nuanced application of an understanding of the brain/mind/body to each of his patient's unique issues.

In summary, neurobiology helps by affirming the brain changing power of the right-brain-to-right-brain attuned dialogue that is at the basis of our nonverbal Bioenergetic approach. This affirmation can support our own security in the therapeutic encounter.

What Neurobiology Does Not Do for Us

So the science, as Dr. Koemeda told us this morning, is fascinating. Marco Iacoboni's book "Mirroring People", describes the way science really happens ... in this instance, the personalities and process that surrounded the discovery in Parma, Italy, of these amazing neurons – it is a really good story. We now know that these neurons are at the base of our imitating, identifying with, and internalizing, and who is to say what discoveries are yet to come?

Drs. Bauer, Arbib, Iacoboni, and Rizzolatti (who is credited with their discovery) have written entire books about Mirror neurons, and there are probably more on the way. There is something truly fascinating about the discovery that there is an area in the brain that, without any effort on our part or even conscious awareness, automatically equips us to read the intention of another person by watching his behavior and simulates the actions and inner state of the person we are observing. It is exciting to see proof that we are equipped to intuit what is going on in another fellow human, that the neural building blocks of the resonance and attunement allow our intimacy with each other, and can be seen lighting up a functional magnetic resonance screen. We know so much more than we did even 10 or 15 years ago.

Yet, there is still so much we do not know about the clinical encounter. Let us be excited by this new knowledge, but let us also stay grounded clinically. First, when I mention mirror neurons, they are obviously not acting alone when they allow us to feel the inner state, emotions and all of a fellow human. Another area, the insula, seems to link the mirror neurons with the limbic system, and the basic functions and rhythms of the body. In other words, as we learned in Bioenergetics "101", we need a resonating body to be attuned and empathic.

Second, the correlations that we see when a research subject does something and a neuroimaging monitor shows a change in activity in a brain area, *are only correlations*. The two events are occurring at the same time, but this does not constitute a proof that one is causing the other. To get closer to such proof, we would have to have the resolution to look at the activity of single cells, but the technology required to do this is unethical in human subjects.

Here is a description by Beatrice Beebe, before motor neurons became so pervasive in clinical research, of what she believes happened for her patient Dolores, while Dolores viewed a video of their therapy process:

> "In watching the video Dolores discovered that I was seeing what she herself 'carried' in her face and body, or 'sensed' about herself, without being able to describe it verbally. Seeing my face seeing her, and hearing my sounds responding to hers, alerted her to her own inner affective reality ... Dolores would find herself 'putting on' my facial expressions while watching the video. By 'wearing' my face Dolores became more affectively aware of her own inner experience, presumably through the proprioceptive feedback of her face ... as well as the feedback from various physiological arousal systems ..."(p. 49).

I am not certain that knowledge of mirror neurons would have enabled Beebe to participate in the described mirroring process more effectively. Perhaps if she had had a patient whose facial expression was quite frozen, and whose limbic system was out to lunch, Beebe would have been sustained by the knowledge that her patient possessed neural hardware, dormant at the moment, but waiting to be quickened.

If our mirror neurons are so smart, why are we so often in the dark about what is going on with our patients? Why are most of us amused, amazed and aghast when our patients tell us how important to them some off-hand gesture or casual comment we made was to them? Often, it was something about our simple humanity ... the people we were before we became wounded healers, that the comment or gesture betrayed to our patient. How much can we ask of our mirror neurons?

First, mirror neurons (and our limbic circuitry) neurons are necessary for our attunement, but they may not be sufficient. Some variety of them may help us to see into the mirrors (eyes) of our patient's soul, but we still have to be able to tolerate what we see in their mirror. We will not be relieved of the struggle to stay present with the patient when what they bring into the room is too intense, not intense enough and/or brings up material in us that is too uncomfortable. Second, we are tough to read. Ekman and Friesen (1980) studied facial emotional expression for decades, and concluded that it is the rare person whose natural intuitive talent enables them to read what is on the heart and mind in the fleeting nuances of facial expression. And, there is projective identification adding a layer of complexity to what the mirror neuron has to decipher.

Then, as Reich (1961) taught us, there is the patient's character armor. Whatever impulses and desires of our patient that were intolerable in his environment, have been unconsciously defended against and disguised. Any specific gesture, or posture of part of the body, may be a complex compromise between core impulses, traumatic experience, and chronic defenses. Finally, there is irony. In Irwin Yalom's wonderful book, *Love's Executioner* (1989), it was the two ironic smiles of his patient that brought home to us the limits of intuition. Each time she smiled, the smile expressed such a nuanced, complex reality within her that no one could possibly grasp its meaning without knowing many interlocking details of her current and past life. So, it remains to be seen if mirror neurons can decipher the array of inner experiences that can lead a person *to smile* or fathom the multiple, contradictory levels of meaning embedded in character structure.

What these neurons actually support is our "implicit relational knowing", (to borrow Lyons-Ruth (1998) apt phrase), which is really a kind of not knowing in the left hemispheric sense. They invite us to trust our intuition, and dwell in the interactive space where what we "know" remains true for only fractions of a second, even as we feel our facial expression mirroring that of our patient. As we were told by the early twentieth century French philosopher, Merleau-Ponty, "I live in the facial expression of the other, as I feel him living in mine" (p. 146). These neurons embolden us to listen more attentively to what comes to us intuitively in fleeting images, whispers, body sensations or fully articulated sentences. I called this "listening with the limbic system" (Lewis, 2004) in an earlier paper of mine. As a bioenergetic therapist over the years, on a good day, I learned to quiet my mind and listen to my hands: they quite often knew where and how I should be touching my patient before I did. Sometimes my hands and I both learned what we should be doing by watching what my patient was doing with his hands.

The above remarks raise the question of whether or not mirror neurons and their like will change the way we teach our craft to our students. This question I cannot answer, other than to wonder with you if the ratio of explicit to implicit will change in our effort to teach expertise in reading the story of a person in the form and motility of their body. And, by the way, when I am trying to get a sense of what is actually going on in the moment in a session, I often explicitly ask my patient how they experienced what just happened. This often seems like a good idea in the moment, but then I realize the potential of the query to pull him out of an important experience for which he has no words, into a premature left hemispheric derailment. How will we teach our students and ourselves when to speak and when to listen to the silence? A Last point on what mirror neurons cannot do for us … and again, I say mirror neurons when I mean the neural systems that enable attuned interactions with our patients. They cannot relieve us the burden of living through the shame, rage and despair in the inevitable enactments with our patients in which we fail them as they once were failed – in which we participate as the old bad object, so that they can revisit the original traumatic failures and perhaps, this time come closer to mastery of them.

In summary, neuroscience has not taken us beyond the ineffable mystery of the clinical encounter. In the next and last section of this paper are two vignettes, which I believe demonstrate that the clinical encounter involves many more variables than can be grasped by mirror neurons or for that matter, be included in an empirical experimental design.

Clinical Vignettes

I am with my patient Marie: Her action, to which my mirror neurons are trying to attune me, is an attempt to express in spoken language a sense of grief about her inability to help her parents to move beyond their highly dysfunctional relationship, both with themselves and Marie herself. My mirror neurons tell me that her voice is quite strangled, and that her words convey little of the unprocessed anguish, shame, and rage that are trapped in the musculature of her neck and throat. These same neurons also allow me to empathically feel Marie's trapped emotions in my own belly and heart – to the extent that is, that I can tolerate them.

I have discovered via trial and error, primarily by asking Marie about her experience of my interventions, that it is most helpful to her if I sit next to her, and stay with the burning ache in my chest as she expresses her grief in the choked vocal timbre that comes over her at such times. I honestly don't know how much my Bioenergetic training has improved on what my mirror neurons (and limbic system) tell me very directly about the emotions and the motoric act, via which she is attempting to communicate with me. Her feelings are deeply entwined with a shameful, traumatic sense of herself as tiny, bleak and unworthy of being known. So I understand that my steady, long-term commitment to witnessing and empathically accompanying her will slowly lead her to a stronger sense of her worth and ability to integrate and reflect on more of the traumatic material from which she has dissociated. I now know that my middle prefrontal cortex and limbic system, figured this out so that *it is they* that know what to do, or more importantly what *not to do* with the information I am getting from my mirror neurons. But before the explosion of neuro-scientific data, we used to call this kind of thoughtful behavior, clinical experience.

A central theme that unites this paper is that there is a complex, but very specific correspondence between the people we therapists are, and the models we offer as explanations for our interventions. This relationship is so complex that I do not believe that the data of neuroscience and our Bioenergetic approach map meaningfully onto each other, unless, that is, the correlations are *anchored in the details of a somatic psychotherapy process.* It is in the spirit of this conclusion, that I offer the vignettes and the discussion that I juxtapose between them.

I grew up with the Reichian amoeba model – that we "trillion-celled" humans, as Lowen wrote, "function on the organismic level as a single cell"(1984, p. 22) … Lowen continues, "on the deepest level, the organismic functions are expansion and contraction, taking in and giving forth" (p. 22). I believe that this model is at the base of how I actually work with my patients.

Yet I hope that my working clinical model actually includes more of the parts of the body that belong to the species that come into my office – that is, homo sapiens, rather than amoebas. Robert Scaer, a neurologist, has developed a sophisticated trauma model in which procedural level neural circuitry acts via a dysregulated autonomic nervous system to cause spastic musculature and illnesses in a variety of the body's end organs. The model is beautiful, although its clinical application is in its infancy.

So, back to the basics, as Dr. Lowen used to say. We come from our core, and when that impulse is frustrated by the environment, we develop armor that traps the impulse and related emotions. When I conduct Bioenergetic therapy I behave as though the emotions/impulses are indeed trapped in the muscles and tissues of the body. If a patient feels a lump forming in his throat or an ache in his heart, I understand that his subjective experience is happening in the physical tissues of his body, and I work with him accordingly.

Dr. Siegel (2011) on the other hand, tells us what any self-respecting neuro-science expert would. He says,

> "neural networks surrounding the hollow organs, such as the intestines and the heart, send complex sensory input to the skull-based brain. This data forms the foundation for visceral maps that help us have a 'Gut feeling' or a 'Heartfelt' sense" (p. 43).

Interestingly, there are quotation marks around gut feeling and heartfelt. I want this paper to inform the reader of how information relevant to our "hands on" approach emerged from the October 2011 IIBA conference at which I read this paper. Robert Hilton, dialoguing with Daniel Siegel on the day following my keynote address, asked him for me whether the quotation marks above suggest the feeling is not actually going on in the body tissues of the gut and heart. Dr. Siegel clarified that he used quotation marks, only because gut feeling and heartfelt are commonplace expressions in our language. While I understood Dr. Siegel's answer, Dr. Hilton asked him another question, the answer to which was harder to understand. Bob's question followed from the vignette in Dr. Siegel's book "Mindfulness", about his patient Stuart. A turning point in Stuart's therapy had occurred when the feeling that he and Dr. Siegel were each held in each other's mind was embodied (made carnate) by Stuart's taking Dr. Siegel's hand in both of his own. Dr. Hilton asked whether touching his patients was part of Dr. Siegel's approach.

Dr. Siegel was quite candid that he found this question challenging, and explained that most of his patients had been either physically or sexually abused, and that for such a population, touch was simply too problematic. However, he continued and I paraphrase, when a patient asks to be hugged at the end of a session, and it seems okay, of course I hug him.

In looking over the 14 vignettes in Dr. Siegel's book, some more detailed than others, I found 4 cases of sexual and/or physical abuse, and a fifth that was unclear. As I said earlier in this paper, we all develop theories/stories that explain our interventions to our patients and ourselves. I experienced Dr. Siegel as an attuned clinician, sensitive to psyche-soma in his way, and appreciative of the conference video of Louise Frechette conducting a Bioenergetic session. But Dr. Siegel would seem to be no exception to a basic thesis in this paper: that the connection between what we do as therapists and the stories with which we explain our actions, is both fascinating and formidably complex. He stresses the centrality of restoring to his patients the experience of their body's aliveness.

And yet, he has his reasons for not concluding that, for a physically and/or sexually abused patient, the experience of safe touch may be a risky, but necessary laying on of hands.

Regarding Bioenergetic therapists, and I hope I am not doing violence to my complexity thesis, I suggest *that something in each of our persons has drawn us to a story in which holding and being held, both in the mind and the body, is at the heart of what is healing.*

I will close with my patient Charles, who is gradually coming down from his mind as the location of his false self, and finally feeling something in his chest and throat. He needs me to hold and be attuned to what he has finally tuned into in himself. In therapy with me for almost 5 years, Charles is 40 years old and, although very high-functioning in his career, he has never had an intimate partner. He is intermittently hypochondriacal and recently had a weeklong episode of chest pain for which no medical cause could be found. He describes his life as a slow-motion panic attack. Standing with knees bent or leaning forward in the basic Bioenergetic grounding position, easily triggers strong dizziness and nausea. Leaning back over the Bioenergetic roller, Charles has on occasion heard the very distant wail of a young child.

Two weeks ago, while lying back over the roller, Charles said he felt like pushing out the "junk" that was inside his belly and chest. I suggested that he try to vocalize a sustained exhalation. As he tried to do so, he felt something moving up the front of his body and getting caught in his throat. For a few seconds I put some pressure on his thyrohyoid membrane – just above his Adam's apple, and with my other hand I pressed down gently on the front of Charles' chest. His voiced exhalation began to come out, and over a period of about a minute, the sound became fuller and there was a rhythmic pulse to it – it pulsated from somewhere deep inside him. The life of his sound and the sound of his life filled the room. After a few minutes, in disbelief, Charles said, "I did not make that sound". He was truly stunned, and as you might say, we (the three of us) sat quietly together, and I was hopeful that Charles was on the verge of becoming intimate with himself.

A week later Charles lay back over the roller and after some time said, "I can't make *that* sound ... I need your help. " He reminded me that, although he did not understand why, what had really relaxed his neck and throat the week before, such that the sound had been able to come out of him, was that I had held and supported his head. So I did so again, and this time the pulsatile sound opened into deep gagging that seemed to come from his diaphragm and solar plexus. The moral, then, of this paper is that sometimes a person really is an amoeba, especially if your therapy involves working with his body.

References

Beebe, B. (2005): Faces-in relation. Forms of intersubjectivity in infant Research and adult treatment. pp. 89–143. New York: Other Press.

Butler, K. (2005): September/October, Psychotherapy Networker: 28.

Ekman, P., Friesen, W., & Ancoli, S. (1980): "Facial signs of emotional Experience." Journal of Personality and Social Psychology, 39, 1125–1134.

Iacoboni, M. (2009): Mirroring People. New York: Picador.

Koemeda, M. (2011): Keynote Address, 21st IIBA International Conference, San Diego, California.

Lewis, R. (1976): "A psychosomatic basis of premature ego development: Infancy and the Head." Energy and Character, Vol. 7 (also on www.bodymindcentral.com).

Lewis, R. (1984): "Cephalic shock as a somatic link to the false self Personality." Comprehensive Psychotherapy, Vol. 4 (also on www.bodymindcentral.com).

Lewis, R. (2004): "Projective identification revisited – Listening with the limbic system." Bioenergetic Analysis, the Clinical Journal of the IIBA, Vol. 14, No. 1.

Lowen, A. (1984): "What is bioenergetic analysis? "Bioenergetic Analysis, the Clinical Journal of the IIBA, Vol. 1, No. 1, pp. 21–28.

Lyons-Ruth, K. (1991): "Rapprochment or aprochment: Mahler's theory reconsidered from the vantage point of recent research on attachment relationships." Psychoanalytic Psychology, Vol. 8.

Lyons-Ruth, K. (1998): "Implicit relational knowing: Its role in development and psychoana-

lytic treatment." Infant Mental Health Journal, Vol. 19, No. 3.
Merleau-Ponty, M.(1964): The Primacy of Perception. Evanston, IL: Northwestern University Press.
Reich, W. (1961/1930): Character Analysis. 3rd enlarged edition. New York: Farrar, Straus & Giroux.
Resneck-Sannes, H. (2007): "The embodied mind." Bioenergetic Analysis, The Clinical Journal of the IIBA, Vol. 17, pp. 39–56.
Scaer, R. (2001): The body bears the burden:trauma, dissociation & disdease. Binghampton, N.Y.: The Haworth Press.
Siegel, D. (2011): Crepes of wrath. Mindsight, pp. 23–37. New York: Bantam books.
Winnicott, D. (1960): "Ego distortion in terms of true and false self.". The Maturational Process and the Facilitating. Environment. pp. 140–152. New York: Int. Univ. Press, 1965.
Winnicott, D (1962): Ego integration in child development. The maturational processes and the facilitating environment. pp. 56–63. New York: Int. Univ. Press, 1965.
Yalom, I. (1989): "Two smiles". Love's Executioner, pp. 167–186. New York: Harper Collins Publishers.

About the Author

Robert Lewis, M.D., in private practice in New York, is a senior trainer on the IIBA faculty, and a member of the clinical faculty of the NYU/Mount Sinai Medical Center. His elucidation of Cephalic Shock and way of working with the head, voice, and diaphragmatic connections to the pelvis, are beyond words. He leads workshops in Europe and the Americas, and residential intensives on Long Island, New York. bodymindcentral.com, docboblewis@gmail.com.

Hans-Jürgen Wirth

9/11 as a Collective Trauma

and other Essays on Psychoanalysis and Society

2004 · 198 pages · hardback
ISBN 978-3-89806-372-2

In 9/11 as a Collective Trauma Hans-Jürgen Wirth presents a collection of his most interesting essays about psyche and politics. He reflects on the psychic structure of suicide bombers and analyzes the psycho-political causes and the consequences of the Iraq War. The other essays focus on xenophobia and violence, the story of Jewish psychoanalysts who emigrated to the United States from Nazi Germany, and the idea of man in psychoanalysis.

Hans-Jürgen Wirth

Narcissism and Power

Psychoanalysis of Mental Disorders in Politics

2009 · 266 pages · hardback
ISBN 978-3-89806-480-4

Social power is irresistibly appealing to narcissistically disturbed personalities. Uninhibited egocentricity, career obsession, a winning mentality and fantasies of grandeur – the narcissist employs these traits to clear the way through the corridors of economic and political power.

Blinded by his fantasies of grandeur and omnipotence, the narcissist loses his grasp on social reality and necessarily fails in the end. It is closely related to this loss of reality that the leader turns away from the norms, values and ideals to which he should actually be committed. Obsession with power, unscrupulousness and cynicism can give rise to brutal misanthropy.

Ralf Vogt

»Beseelbare« Therapy Objects

Psychoanalytic interactional approach in a body- and trauma-oriented psychotherapy

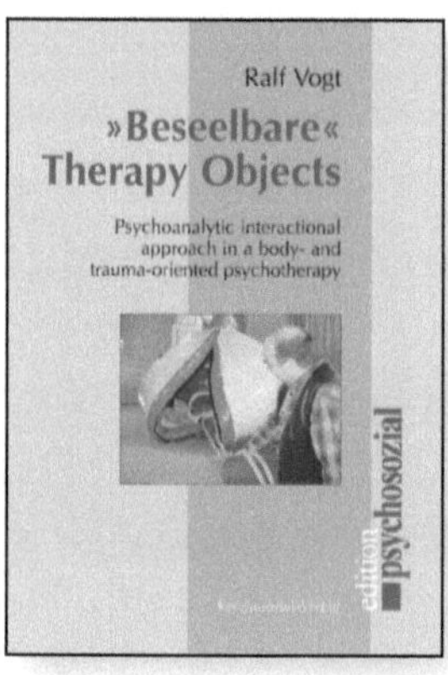

2006 · 187 pages · paperback
ISBN 978-3-89806-700-3

Ralf Vogt presents a new form of body therapy which may be applied as individual and as group psychotherapy. The core of his original concept are »›beseelbare‹ objects«. With the help of such objects, typical conflict situations may be performed and problem-specific solutions may be playfully tested. The objects used to that end – for example a cuddly cave into which the patient may crawl – were specifically designed for psychotherapeutic work by the author. These »›beseelbare‹ therapy objects« are an important aid to get access to any blocked or buried affects of the patients.

Ralf Vogt

Psychotrauma, State, Setting

Psychoanalytical-Action-Related Model for a Treatment of Complexly Traumatized Patients (SPIM-20-CTP)

2008 · 337 pages · paperback
ISBN 978-3-89806-871-0

Ralf Vogt presents a complete conception of a psychotraumatological treatment which is applicable to complex traumatized patients (representing the majority of psychotrauma disorders in ambulant practices) as well as to other patients. His very structured procedure with theoretical derivations, including many handouts for clients and treaters, and specific case vignettes, is unique and important in its compactness to the point of evaluation. The book is suitable reading for therapists and advisors, and also for advanced patients.

www.ingramcontent.com/pod-product-compliance
Ingram Content Group UK Ltd.
Pitfield, Milton Keynes, MK11 3LW, UK
UKHW040026200726
13854UKWH00001B/389

9 783837 921595